Benevolence

Benevolence

MORRIS PANYCH

Talonbooks

Copyright © 2008 Morris Panych

Talonbooks
P.O. Box 2076, Vancouver, British Columbia, Canada V6B 3S3
www.talonbooks.com

Typeset in Méridien and Frutiger and printed and bound in Canada.

First Printing: 2008

The publisher gratefully acknowledges the financial support of the Canada Council for the Arts; the Government of Canada through the Book Publishing Industry Development Program; and the Province of British Columbia through the British Columbia Arts Council and the Book Publishing Tax Credit for our publishing activities.

No part of this book, covered by the copyright hereon, may be reproduced or used in any form or by any means—graphic, electronic or mechanical—without prior permission of the publisher, except for excerpts in a review. Any request for photocopying of any part of this book shall be directed in writing to Access Copyright (The Canadian Copyright Licensing Agency), 1 Yonge Street, Suite 800, Toronto, Ontario, Canada M5E 1E5; tel.: (416) 868-1620; fax: (416) 868-1621.

Rights to produce *Benevolence*, in whole or in part, in any medium by any group, amateur or professional, are retained by the author. Interested persons are requested to contact the Gary Goddard Agency, 305–10 St. Mary Street, Toronto, Ontario, Canada M4Y 1P9; tel.:(416) 928-0299; fax: (416) 924-9593; e-mail: goddard@canadafilm.com.

Library and Archives Canada Cataloguing in Publication

Panych, Morris
    Benevolence / Morris Panych.

A play.
ISBN 978-0-88922-584-8

    I. Title.
PS8581.A65B45 2008   C812'.54   C2008-901050-7

To my mother, Rosemary Adele, who passed away in September; a woman deeply concerned with and dedicated to the lives of those less fortunate.

Benevolence was first performed at Tarragon Theatre,
Toronto, Ontario, September 24, 2007.

Written and Directed by Morris Panych
Set and Costume Design by Ken MacDonald
Lighting Design by Andrea Lundy
Original Music and Sound Design by Thomas Ryder Payne

Cast

PATRON Colin Heath
TERENCE LOMY Stephen Ouimette
OSWALD EICHERSEN Tom Rooney
AUDREY Jennifer Wigmore
JACKIE Gina Wilkinson

Management and Crew

Stage Manager Maria Popoff
Apprentice Stage Manager Lindsay Marriner
Fight Director John Stead
Script Coordinator Margaret Thompson
Mainspace Technician Veronica Good
Production Manager Michael Freeman
Technical Director Chris Carlton
Interim Technical Director Doug Morum
Head of Properties Monique Stewart
Head Carpenter Ian Chappell
Head Scenic Artist Lindsay Anne Black

Head of Wardrobe	Chloë Anderson
Photographer	Cylla von Tiedemann
Graphic Designer	Kilby Smith-McGregor
Assistant Carpenters	Kevin Hutson
	Al Gullion
Assistant Scenic Artists	Jeremy Smith
	Amanda White
Carpentry Crew	Shanna Miller
	Daniel McIlmoyl
	Kate McKay
	Veronica Good
	J.Louis Berenguer
	Sarah-Jane Patterson
	Shannon Lintott
Wigs and Make-up	Sharon Ryman
Production Assistant	Emma Laird
Lighting Crew	Kevin Hutson
	Shanna Miller
	Daniel McIlmoyl
	Kate McKay
	Caitlyn Weld
	Virginia Good

Setting

The action of the play takes place in a tiny, shabby, old movie theatre—the type of venue for second-rate porn films. Some scenes happen during a film, when the lighting indicates a picture is in progress; mostly, though, the screen is blank and the houselights up, to reveal the prevailing decrepitude.

Scene One

As the play begins, OSWALD EICHERSEN enters. Watching from a seat in the back corner of the theatre is TERENCE LOMY. EICHERSEN is a forty-something man in a cheap business suit. He tries discreetly to find a seat. He sits and watches the film with a certain detached curiosity. Somewhere between him and LOMY sits a regular PATRON, who moves, now and again, sitting near to others, in the fashion of a discreet wanker—the type one might expect to find in this sort of place. At one point, all three viewers crane their heads sideways to understand the angle of a particular shot; moans emanate from the screen, interspersed with garbled dialogue. After a bit of this, LOMY moves down the aisle and sits a row behind EICHERSEN, to one side. LOMY is a street person, dressed in tattered clothes. His hair is matted and tied to one side with a small pink ribbon. He wears cotton gardening gloves and hasn't shaved in while. He has that kind of sun-beaten complexion one expects from people who sleep over a sewer grate in all seasons.

LOMY
    Hi.

EICHERSEN
    Good grief.

LOMY
    I didn't mean to frighten you.

EICHERSEN
    You didn't.

LOMY
    I didn't mean to.

EICHERSEN
>   I'm not frightened.

>> *The pair sits in silence for a bit, craning their necks some more as they watch the film. The regular PATRON moves again, a little closer.*

LOMY
>   You know, I think I've seen this before.

>> *Beat.*

EICHERSEN
>   I don't mean to be—um, uh—I don't—

LOMY

>> *Lunging forward, leaning over the back of the seat next to EICHERSEN.*

>   Popcorn?

EICHERSEN
>   Just ... What?—no, thank you—

LOMY
>   It's not very good.

EICHERSEN
>   What, uh, what is it you want, Mr. uh, Mr.—?

LOMY
>   Lomy. But call me Terence. I was named after my father. Apparently.

EICHERSEN
>   Were you?

LOMY
>   Apparently.

>> *The film ends, and the lights come on. The regular PATRON, lowering his hat, gathers a couple of bags and exits, quietly, if clumsily.*

>   You have a piece of fluff on your jacket there. May I take that off?

EICHERSEN
I don't—I can do that, thank you—Mr.—Lomy?

LOMY
Terence, if we're going to be friends.

EICHERSEN
Well, that's—that's—yes, that's ... Look, I don't use people's first names, generally. It seems a little informal when you don't really know the person. For example, the way I really, the way I really don't know you.

LOMY
You know me.

EICHERSEN
Not—that's the—thing: not really. Not—

LOMY
This is the third time we've met.

EICHERSEN
I was, yes, I was getting to that. I thought I—I told you yesterday that I—I told you yesterday that I didn't need to have a meeting with you. If I'd needed to have a meeting with you, I would have; I would have had one then and there, in the hallway.

LOMY
I prefer to call it a rendezvous.

Beat.

EICHERSEN
Let's not get bogged down with semantics at this point. Let's just—

LOMY
Sure, OK.

EICHERSEN
What were we talking about?

LOMY
Let's wait 'til we're alone.

EICHERSEN
> We are alone.

>> *LOMY gets up and moves to EICHERSEN's row, now sitting directly beside him.*

LOMY
> Hi. Yeah, obviously we couldn't have a rendezvous in your apartment building, Mr. Eichersen. That would be an imposition on you. I didn't want this to be an imposition, and if you want to call it a meeting, well, I can live with that. I can.

EICHERSEN
> Imposition? You're not serious. You've called my number thirty times in the past twenty-four hours. Imposition is a—that's a—that's a ... Where did you get my number?

LOMY
> Has it, has it been that many times? Thirty.

EICHERSEN
> You had me paged at work.

LOMY
> Listen, it wasn't a problem.

EICHERSEN
> No?

LOMY
> There's a free phone at the clinic. I just wanted to make sure you got the message. About the rendezvous. This is not a well-known venue.

EICHERSEN
> Really.

LOMY
> Here.

>> *Handing EICHERSEN a five.*

EICHERSEN
> What's this?

LOMY
The money you left at the box office. You didn't notice she was asleep?

He tucks the money into EICHERSEN's pocket.

She's always asleep.

EICHERSEN
That's—dishonest.

LOMY
Yeah, I don't know how they make any money here, frankly. They used to show Kurosawa. I don't know when they started this porn thing. I find it interesting that people would gather together in groups for such a solitary purpose, if you know what I'm saying.

EICHERSEN
It's not even porn. I think they were actually trying to string a story together there: sort of softcore comedy. Not funny *and* not dirty.

LOMY
Try not to be so judgmental.

EICHERSEN
What?

LOMY
It's unlike you.

EICHERSEN
As a matter of fact, it's very like me; I can be quite— critical of screenplays, for your information, having not— yet—written a successful one myself, apparently.

Beat.

I'm sorry, I don't know why that came up.

LOMY
Yeah, neither do I.

EICHERSEN
> But at least you'll find, in my pathetic and vain attempts at the medium, a story, somewhere—

LOMY
> Uh-huh.

EICHERSEN
> Emerges—

LOMY
> You like a story—a plot; I get it, sure.

EICHERSEN
> This has got nothing to do with anything.

LOMY
> Everything has to do with everything.

EICHERSEN
> Oh. Is that—?
>
> > *Beat.*
>
> How do you know what's unlike me?

LOMY
> I don't; it's true. You're an intensely private person. And why is that? Why so private? Who knows? Maybe you don't want to get into that right now. Wait. OK. No. Let's dare to broach the subject once and for all. Let's roll up our sleeves a little here.

EICHERSEN
> What subject?

LOMY
> The subject of why you aren't more outgoing. You don't have what I'd call a great personality, true, but you have a good personality. You should let it shine.

EICHERSEN
> Shine?

LOMY
It's a corny idea, but you know a smile can be infectious. Infectious.

EICHERSEN
No it can't.

LOMY
Here. Try it.

He tries to make a smile on EICHERSEN's face.

EICHERSEN
I don't—smile; it's a family tradition.

LOMY
Can I be honest?

EICHERSEN
No.

LOMY
You're afraid of who you really are; that's my theory.

EICHERSEN
Oh, is that, is that—? Uh-huh? That's your theory, is it?

LOMY
And occasionally, when you finally—yes, my theory—when you do something truly wonderful, like the other day—

EICHERSEN
Can we forget about the other day? It didn't happen.

LOMY
Don't try to hide it. Don't. We know.

EICHERSEN
No, we don't.

LOMY
It's a part of you. A kind and wonderful you that's just busting to get out of this—phony exterior.

EICHERSEN
Please don't—touch me. That's ... Phony?

LOMY
You're a very complicated person.

EICHERSEN
I don't want anything busting out. I don't; I—

LOMY
Then why did you give me that money?

EICHERSEN
Does there have to be a reason?

LOMY
Yes. I don't know. You tell me.

EICHERSEN
If there's a reason for everything, then, then why are you so down on your luck?
Sorry.

LOMY
We'd have to look a lot deeper, I think, to answer that question. We'd have to look at the whole nature of modern capitalism, and I'm not sure this is the time or place for that. Besides, what's your measure of success?

EICHERSEN
Well—it would probably have something to do with not living on a piece of cardboard, outside my building.

LOMY
I see.

EICHERSEN
I'm sorry; that was—I don't think there's a reason for anything.

LOMY
This is interesting. You're challenging me, philosophically. We're engaging in a kind of polemic.

EICHERSEN
I'm saying maybe things just happen—out of the blue, without reason, no sense to them. Things, for example, that you later regret.

LOMY
> You don't regret giving me the money if that's where you're headed with this.

EICHERSEN
> I—no, I don't regret it. Of course I don't regret it.

LOMY
> You're so—sweet.

EICHERSEN
> Stop it; I don't need a massage at the moment, thank you.

LOMY
> Twice I tried to—*relax*—tried to return it, but you wouldn't take it.

EICHERSEN
> I don't want to relax.

LOMY
> It wasn't a mistake. That was you. A hundred dollars. That was the real Mr. Eichersen. *A hundred dollars.*

EICHERSEN
> Stop using my name. Stop—touching me and stop using my name.

LOMY
> What's your screenplay about?

EICHERSEN
> What? Nothing. OK, so it was the real me. Let's say, for instance.

LOMY
> It's about nothing?

EICHERSEN
> Then, *fine*. I'm satisfied and you're satisfied. And you're a hundred dollars richer, and I'm a hundred dollars poorer.

LOMY
> I bet it's not about nothing.

EICHERSEN
You don't need to thank me anymore. I consider myself thanked, and you're welcome. You're very, very welcome.

LOMY
You know there's more to it than that.

EICHERSEN
Let go of my arm.

LOMY
I'm not letting go.

EICHERSEN
Let go.

LOMY
It's not very often that something happens in your life. I mean, *happens*.

EICHERSEN
No?

LOMY holds him a little too tightly.

LOMY
I've been hanging out on that corner for two years. No one has given me more than a quarter at any given time. Alright, there was a guy who gave me a coupon to a Bar-B-Que ribs place, which I have to say didn't live up to the hyperbole; and a woman, once, gave me her engagement ring, but that was only out of anger and the fiancé took it right back. But in all the time I have been on that corner, Mr. Eichersen, nobody, nobody, *nobody*—nobody, *nobody*, has given me anything that wasn't easy for them to part with.

He lets go of EICHERSEN's arm; although disengaged, the threat remains tangible.

EICHERSEN
Like I said, it was sort of—a—

LOMY
Don't say it was a mistake. You can't do that.

EICHERSEN
> Well, alright. Let's call it a lapse.

LOMY
> See. This is what you always do. You understate things.

EICHERSEN
> How do you know that? If anything, I overstate them, a little.

LOMY
> Don't get me wrong. I think humility has its place.

EICHERSEN
> Listen. It's possible to do things that aren't part of your personality. Impulses. Certain impulses. Like wanting to leap in front of a subway.

LOMY
> You know what? I've had that, too.

EICHERSEN
> Well, fine. So, you know. It's not necessarily something you're going to do. Or maybe it is something you're going to do. When you get around to it.

LOMY
> I don't think that's what happened, Mr. Eichersen. Can I call you Oswald?

EICHERSEN
> Have you—? Alright, I'm sorry to ask this—because I don't mean to imply, by asking this, that you are a, a criminal, in any way—just, just because you're a panhandler.

LOMY
> Is that what you think I am? A panhandler?

EICHERSEN
> I'm sorry, is there another name for it?

LOMY
> I'm just messing with you.

EICHERSEN
Did you happen to steal my wallet? Yesterday? Sorry. I just had to ask.

LOMY
Happen—to steal? I think if I was going to steal your wallet, I wouldn't *happen* to; I just fucking would.

EICHERSEN
So, how did you find out my name?

LOMY
Is that why you agreed to meet me?

EICHERSEN
Well, no. I wanted to, wanted to—

LOMY
Something nice happens between us, and now you want to—make it not nice. Accusing me—

EICHERSEN
I'm not accusing you.

LOMY
OK.

EICHERSEN
It's just that my wallet is missing—

LOMY
OK, what is a wallet?

EICHERSEN
Uh—

LOMY
So, this is the measure of a man, now. You take away his wallet, what is he? Quite frankly, it sickens me. Yeah, I took your wallet. Because I wanted to prove something to you. I wanted to show you how kindness is a two-way street, Oswald.

EICHERSEN
OK.

LOMY
You did a good thing, and now I get to do one.

He hands EICHERSEN his wallet.

That could have been somebody else who took that, and I don't mean somebody else. You know what I'm saying?

EICHERSEN
Not—

LOMY
I mean, me. I mean, before. You changed me. Your magnanimity has ignited me. I am ignited, man. I don't know what I'm going to do next.

EICHERSEN
Hopefully not—pick my pocket.

LOMY
This was just a little gesture: a reciprocation.

EICHERSEN doesn't know what to say.

It could have been some other guy who got that hundred bucks. Some less observant type of person who might not have noticed it for the gesture that it was. A calling out.

EICHERSEN
Look. I'm not calling out, as you say, and that I can tell you for certain. I have a psychiatrist who accuses me of that already. And I'm not. If I was calling out I would—*call out*.

LOMY
You don't need a psychiatrist. Do you really need a psychiatrist?

EICHERSEN
What? Yes. No. Yes. Of course not "need"—not need, in the sense of have to have. Do I need some sanctimonious bastard criticizing my decisions by stopping his pen from writing suddenly and lifting the nib off the paper, just ever-so-slightly, as some kind of, kind of silent commentary on my personal choices, to the point where

I'm afraid to utter my real thoughts, so I invent fake ones that I know he'll approve of? Just so he won't stop writing? Just so we can carry on with the session without anything of interest happening, and I can get back to my life without having to divest myself of what little dignity I have left? Why am I telling you this?

LOMY
Why are you telling me this?

EICHERSEN
Listen. Let's just roll the clock back twenty-four hours. I'm walking home, OK?

LOMY
OK.

EICHERSEN
Rounding the corner, I see you—

LOMY
You see me—

EICHERSEN
I nod my head, oh, I think, I'm going to give this man a hundred dollars, just because I feel like it; no other reason—

LOMY
No other reason, exactly.

EICHERSEN
Because I feel like it, that's all.

LOMY
That's it.

EICHERSEN
But then, no, suddenly, I stop. *No.* This is just one of those crazy impulses of mine, and, according to Dr. Strauss, I need to check those impulses because, because they're just impulses and, anyway, lots of people think about terrible things and crazy things and never do them and besides, "Routine is good, routine is normal." So, I stick to the routine. I walk by. Just the way I have every other

day for the past two years. Nothing changes; we go back to our completely unconnected lives of mutual disregard.

LOMY
It's almost touching, this desperate attempt of yours to seem not nice all of a sudden. But I'm not buying it.

EICHERSEN
No?

LOMY
You can't make me think you're not nice. You're not not nice. I don't like double negatives, but sometimes there's just no other way to put things.

EICHERSEN
You know what I did, once? I kicked a dog.

LOMY
Is that right.

EICHERSEN
A perfectly—yes—nice, perfectly sweet little pug-nosed dog.

LOMY
Those yappy little fuckers with the pushed-in faces?

EICHERSEN
With the—yes.

LOMY
Who could blame you?

EICHERSEN
But in this case it was my girlfriend's dog. When she was out of the room, I kicked it. So, you see? You see?

LOMY
Maybe you don't like your girlfriend.

EICHERSEN
Why wouldn't I? She's perfect. She's the top commercial real estate saleswoman in her office.

LOMY
: And you resent her; I get it. Fucking women.

EICHERSEN
: I don't, I don't, I don't resent her. Not when I can take it out on her ugly little dog, or in other ways, like, like using words I know she hates: "presently" and "picayune." Or purposely ordering the wrong pizza, and pretending it was a mistake. How's that for a nice person?

LOMY
: Even good people do bad things. That isn't what qualifies you. What qualifies you is what's in your heart.

EICHERSEN
: There's nothing in my heart. I don't have a heart. I'm a complete subhuman anomaly. I don't even like my mother.

LOMY
: Yes, you do.

EICHERSEN
: I don't. I'm going to have her committed to a mental institution.

LOMY
: Is she insane?

EICHERSEN
: Yes. No. Yes, she's insane; except that I'm the only one who can see it, apparently. She washes used plastic wrap and hangs it out to dry, then puts it back on the roll. She's used the same roll for fifteen years. This is a woman who named her own son Oswald, but insists on calling him Michael. Why? I don't know. But it doesn't help my feelings of distance and inadequacy, I have to tell you.

LOMY
: You should talk to her about that.

EICHERSEN
: That would mean I had to talk to her. I don't talk to her.

LOMY
Why not? She's your mother.

EICHERSEN
She signed me up for flamenco lessons. What is she doing?

LOMY
Maybe she sees potential.

EICHERSEN
Why am I talking to you about this? I don't want to talk to you about this.

LOMY
Maybe you do: as a friend. Maybe that's what this is all about. Don't you get it? Two guys, alone in the world? Suddenly, not alone? Or at least together in their aloneness? Now that's a story.

EICHERSEN
You're not my friend. Let's get that—out of the way. Let's —I'm sorry. You're not.

LOMY
I understand.

EICHERSEN
Do you?

LOMY
I understand.

EICHERSEN
Good. So, we can go back to our—old relationship. In other words, no relationship.

LOMY
Sure. I get it.

Beat. As LOMY tries not to be hurt, EICHERSEN writhes a little with feelings of guilt.

EICHERSEN
Are you being—is this—?

LOMY
    I'm fine.

EICHERSEN
    I just—I felt more comfortable, somehow, knowing, well, knowing that you don't care about me one way or the other.

LOMY
    You would be wrong about that, but fine. I don't feel hurt by your rejection.

EICHERSEN
    This is not rejection. Rejection implies that there was something there in the first place.

LOMY
    Sure.

EICHERSEN
    You can't say you care about me. You don't know me.

LOMY
    I've been on that corner for two years. You pass by every day and pretend to ignore me. That isn't nothing. That's a lot of pretending.

EICHERSEN
    I'm not pretending.

        Beat.

    This is some sort of social commentary, isn't it? You're trying to make some kind of social commentary. We are not together in our aloneness or anything like that. I am alone in my aloneness.

LOMY
    Not if you give me a hundred dollars.

EICHERSEN
    Here's how that happened, OK. Just so we can end the speculation. As I rounded the corner, and I saw you there for the umpteenth time, with your supercilious grin, and that sleeping bag, that filthy—that—and the cardboard

sign about being hungry, which offends me deeply because it's so manipulative, and patently false because anybody can get a meal in this town if they really want it; and so I saw you standing there and I thought to myself, "If I gave this man enough money, would he go away forever, and leave me alone? Because frankly, frankly I'm sick of having to step over a homeless person going to and from my stinking, boring job that is, to me, a living hell, but I do anyway, because I have a sense of personal responsibility, which clearly this man lacks." So, I thought, "What would it cost to make him disappear from my conscience, so at least I wouldn't feel like such a loser for actually working for a living at such a hateful, tedious job? While people sit in the street with signs draped around their necks, resenting me, and implying, in some backhanded way, that I don't care about them." Does that explain it?

LOMY
I never resented you.

EICHERSEN
That's a lie.

LOMY
I felt sorry for you on occasion, but I never resented you.

EICHERSEN
And why would you feel sorry for me?

LOMY
I know it's hard out there in the business world—

EICHERSEN
Oh, do you.

LOMY
Yes, I know how frustrating and difficult it can be; and it must be terribly galling to have a guy hanging around on your street with no intention of ever moving because he feels fine just where he is.

EICHERSEN backs down a little.

EICHERSEN
It's not my street, it's everybody's street.

LOMY
If I was you, I would have punched my fucking face in. I would have kicked me in the side of the head.

EICHERSEN
Let's—not get carried away.

LOMY
I'm serious. I haven't got any patience for guys like me. None.

EICHERSEN
Now you're being—is this supposed to be ironic?

LOMY
No.

EICHERSEN
Our society is supposed to be tolerant of certain things.

LOMY
Tolerant?

EICHERSEN
We don't punch people out for being poor, or kick them gleefully in the side of the head; that would be—it wouldn't be much of a social arrangement.

LOMY
Why not?

EICHERSEN
You're having me on.

LOMY
Am I?

EICHERSEN
You're playing some sort of weird head game with me. I have to go.

LOMY
>	I'm serious. I don't think people should be hanging out on the streets, begging for money.

EICHERSEN
>	Well, of course not. They should be taken care of: by the state. Everybody should be taken care of. That's the—isn't that the—?

LOMY
>	Why? People who can't take care of themselves shouldn't expect other people to do it for them.

EICHERSEN
>	I can't tell when you're being serious and when you're not.

LOMY
>	You need to get to know me a little better.

EICHERSEN
>	I don't want to know you.

LOMY
>	Look, I'll see you tomorrow.

EICHERSEN
>	No, you won't.

LOMY
>	I'll see you tomorrow, Oswald. Everything's going to be fine. I'm taking care of my little buddy from now on.

EICHERSEN
>	I'll call the police and have you arrested. I'm sorry, but if it comes to that, I'll have you arrested. I'm not your little buddy.

LOMY
>	You can't have me arrested; you wouldn't. What for?

EICHERSEN
>	I don't know. Something. Some—harassment thing.

LOMY
>	It's just not like you.

EICHERSEN
No? You don't know what I'm capable of.

LOMY
I know what you're capable of. And I know what I'm capable of.

EICHERSEN hears this.

EICHERSEN
Meaning?

LOMY produces a knife.

LOMY
Hey. Know what this is, Oswald?

EICHERSEN
I don't—that's a—it's a—

LOMY
It's an instrument of advancement is what it is. It moves our relationship forward a little.

EICHERSEN
It's a—knife.

LOMY
That's right, little buddy; it's a knife.

EICHERSEN
What are you—planning to do with it?

LOMY
I don't really know, man. Maybe I was coming in here to hurt you. Maybe you were the last fucking straw. You know?

EICHERSEN
Is that—?

LOMY
We don't know what we're going to do. Sometimes, we just do it.

EICHERSEN
So—

LOMY
>And sometimes, we don't.

>>*Puts the knife away.*

>You know what I'm talking about?

EICHERSEN
>No.

LOMY
>I'm talking about changes. You, me—

EICHERSEN
>I see.

LOMY
>Do you?

EICHERSEN
>Not really.

LOMY
>Look at you; you're so paranoid. Hey, a guy like me can be a generous guy, too. He just has a different way of giving.

>>*Beat.*

>Relax. I'll see you tomorrow.

>>*EICHERSEN looks at him. LOMY rises from his seat, hands EICHERSEN the rest of his popcorn, and exits the theatre. Blackout.*

Scene Two

> *EICHERSEN is seated in the theatre once again. He is clearly angry as he looks straight ahead at the screen. He looks at his watch, continues with the film, etc. The regular PATRON is seated at the back, as usual, making a bit of noise.*

EICHERSEN
 Must you do that?

> *The PATRON slumps down into a seat, putting on a surgical mask. In a moment, LOMY enters and makes his way down the aisle to sit beside EICHERSEN.*

LOMY
 Hey.

EICHERSEN
 Where have you been?

LOMY
 Have I missed much?

EICHERSEN
 You've kept me waiting an hour.

LOMY
 Have I?

> *The PATRON moves away a little.*

EICHERSEN
 And must we meet *here*?

LOMY
 You're angry. Look at you. Don't be angry.

EICHERSEN
   I'm not angry. I'm being completely rational. See? Rational.

LOMY
   You know, I think you should have your cholesterol checked. Do you have regular cholesterol readings?

EICHERSEN
   (*livid*) Cholesterol.

LOMY
   Let me check your glands.

EICHERSEN
   My glands don't need checking. My glands are fine. Don't—

LOMY
   I know a herbalist. Well, alright, he's a drug dealer. But with holistic credentials.

EICHERSEN
   What did you say to my girlfriend?

LOMY
   Your girlfriend?

EICHERSEN
   Yes, Audrey. What did you say to her?

LOMY
   Nothing.

EICHERSEN
   In the note. You left her a note. With the dog.

LOMY
   Dog?

EICHERSEN
   Don't play games with me.

LOMY
I'm not playing any games. Drink?

He produces a bottle wrapped in a bag.

EICHERSEN
No.

LOMY
It's non-alcoholic.

EICHERSEN
Why have you got it in a paper bag?

LOMY
If people knew it was orange juice, it might upset their sense of moral balance.

Beat of silence. LOMY drinks.

EICHERSEN
You murdered her dog.

LOMY
What?

EICHERSEN
You murdered Audrey's dog.

LOMY
Why would I murder a dog?

EICHERSEN
You tell me.

LOMY
Look, what happened was, things got carried through to their logical conclusion; that's all.

EICHERSEN
Logical what?

LOMY
Conclusion. Well, OK, not a conclusion; let's call it a development. You hated that dog.

EICHERSEN
What difference does that make?

LOMY
Action. That's what's missing in your life, Oswald.

EICHERSEN
I don't want action in my life. Action?

LOMY
Fine. Then what are you doing here?

EICHERSEN
What am I doing here?

LOMY
Why don't you go to the police?

EICHERSEN
That is a very good question.

LOMY
We both know the answer.

EICHERSEN
Do we.

LOMY
Tell me. How did you honestly feel when you found out that stupid little dog was dead? Honestly. Come now. If you could see yourself right now; I just love you when you're like this. Tell me you weren't gratified, when you found out. That dog had no right to exist. That dog stood in the way of your happiness. Why should anything stand in the way of your happiness?

EICHERSEN
I'll tell you why.

LOMY
Alright.

The film ends.

Wait; I just want to see the credits here for a second.

They watch the credits roll.

I *thought* that was her.

EICHERSEN
Who?

LOMY
She starred in *Down Under*.

EICHERSEN
Did she.

LOMY
Featured anyway. She has a very distinct vocal cadence; don't you think?

EICHERSEN
She spoke?

LOMY
So. Happiness.

EICHERSEN
What?

LOMY
You were going to explain to me why something should stand in the way of your happiness. I don't think so. Let's discuss it.

EICHERSEN
It's, it's—possible, in fact it's probable—

LOMY
Probable, uh-huh.

EICHERSEN
That people weren't meant to be happy. That their lives are constructed in a more complicated, more perplexing way. Happiness is a phony idea, invented by—invented by—salesmen, like the ones I work with.

Beat.

LOMY
Is that?—OK, are you finished?

EICHERSEN
> Yes, why?

LOMY
> I'm just surprised you ended a sentence with a preposition.

EICHERSEN
> Happiness is a mirage.

LOMY
> Isn't that a bit cynical? Even for a screenwriter?

EICHERSEN
> I'm not a screenwriter.

LOMY
> Yes, you are.

> *The PATRON exits.*

EICHERSEN
> Let's just, let's address this, this concept of happiness.

LOMY
> I like it when you're like this. I like it when you express yourself.

EICHERSEN
> It's unreasonable to expect everything to work out exactly the way you hoped.

LOMY
> Uh-huh.

EICHERSEN
> That said, my happiness, in any case, whatever it may entail, is not, nor was it ever, predicated on the poisoning of an innocent, albeit annoying, little dog.

LOMY
> Not predicated, no. But it's gone, now. And things are so much better. Look how much better they are.

EICHERSEN
> Not with my girlfriend, they're not.

LOMY
Stop saying "girlfriend." You don't even like her, really.

EICHERSEN
How do you know?

LOMY
When was the last time you had sex with her?

EICHERSEN
Sex?

LOMY
I rest my case.

EICHERSEN
Did you know that there is a law against killing animals? There's an actual law.

LOMY
You know what the law is? The law is a line in the middle of the road. OK? A *line*: in the middle of the fucking road. You *are* the road.

EICHERSEN
You have committed a criminal offence. You could go to jail. Only, of course, I'll be the one going to jail, because you signed the note from me. That's—thanks—very helpful.

LOMY
I only did what I had to do. As your friend; as your agent.

EICHERSEN
Agent?

LOMY
Listen. Can we talk about all this later?

EICHERSEN
No.

LOMY
I'd love to continue this discourse with you, I really would—

EICHERSEN
   I want to talk about it now. I want you out of my life. Now.

LOMY
   No you don't. You're just upset. It takes time to adjust to these things.

EICHERSEN
   What things?

   LOMY rises to go.

   Mr. Lomy, I want you to stay right here. I want you to sit down and wait with me. I asked Audrey to meet us here at three o'clock—

LOMY
   You asked her to meet you at a porn theatre?

EICHERSEN
   I suggested a coffee shop. You said it wasn't your milieu.

LOMY
   I didn't say "milieu." I think I said "cup of tea." I think that's funnier, don't you? Coffee isn't my cup of tea. I think it's funnier.

EICHERSEN
   I want you to sit here and look her straight in the eye and tell her it was you who poisoned her dog, and it was you who wrote the note that was stapled to the dog's nose, and that I had nothing to do with any of this—nothing. Whatsoever. Do you hear me?

LOMY
   I can't do that.

EICHERSEN
   You can and you will.

LOMY
   I have to hook up with some people. There's a lot going on. I'll see you later.

EICHERSEN
    You won't see me later. I'm going to the police. Come back here. Come back. What people?

    LOMY exits down the aisle just as JACKIE enters; they pass. JACKIE, a somewhat haggard girl, dressed in a very short skirt, continues down the aisle until she finds EICHERSEN, who sits, fuming.

JACKIE
    Ozzie?

EICHERSEN
    Sorry?

    She moves in and sits beside him.

JACKIE
    Hey. Hi. So. What's up?

EICHERSEN
    I beg your pardon?

JACKIE
    Take it easy, honey; relax.

EICHERSEN
    I don't want to relax. Why is everybody so anxious for me to relax? Honey? I'm perfectly—Who are you?

JACKIE
    Jackie.

EICHERSEN
    Do I know you?

JACKIE
    You've seen me around.

EICHERSEN
    I have?

JACKIE
    At the Superdrugs. Outside, mostly—by the exit. Recognize this patented move?

    She does her patented move.

EICHERSEN
　Uh—

JACKIE
　It looks much better under the neon.

EICHERSEN
　That's, well—

JACKIE
　Eh?

EICHERSEN
　Mm.

JACKIE
　So, yeah.

EICHERSEN
　So, what, what can I do for you?

JACKIE
　That is so sweet. Lomy was right. You ask what you can do for me just like that, out of the blue. "What can I do for you?" That is—so fucking considerate. People are such pricks; such pricks in this world, Ozzie. Can I call you that? These shoes are killing me.

EICHERSEN
　He told you my name.

JACKIE
　Look, I don't as a general policy blow people—

EICHERSEN
　Blow people? In what sense? Oh. *Oh*. Uh—

JACKIE
　Yeah, because of my recurring gingivitis—but I can give you a hand job, if that's—

EICHERSEN
　A—ha—

JACKIE
> Don't think of it as a consolation, by any means. I have a somewhat famous technique.

EICHERSEN
> Famous, is it? That's very—that's—I don't want a hand job; thank you. What is this? Please.

JACKIE
> Lomy said you could use the release.

EICHERSEN
> Oh, did he.

JACKIE
> Anyway, it's on the house.

EICHERSEN
> It is.

JACKIE
> Just don't tell Archie.

EICHERSEN
> And who's he?

JACKIE
> You know.

EICHERSEN
> No, I don't know. Your boyfriend?

JACKIE
> You should part your hair differently.

EICHERSEN
> Why?

JACKIE
> It makes your face too symmetrical.

EICHERSEN
> I like symmetry.

JACKIE
> I can tell.

EICHERSEN
What's wrong with symmetry?

JACKIE
It lacks movement. Hair should have movement.

EICHERSEN
Uh, please; my hair is fine. It doesn't like going places. Thank you. If you'll excuse me—

JACKIE
Where are you going, baby?

EICHERSEN
Going? I'm going. I'm—

JACKIE
You don't like me, or what?

EICHERSEN
I don't—know you. I like you as much as I like anybody.

JACKIE
That's so nice.

EICHERSEN
Is it?

JACKIE
I'm Jackie. You've seen me around. You even looked me over a couple of times. I used to be on the opposite corner to the Mr. Tasty, by the twenty-four-hour cheque cashing place; but I got a demotion.

EICHERSEN
Sorry to hear that.

JACKIE
One time you cashed a cheque in there and when you came out, it was raining, I remember, and I said, "Have a nice day," like that. I had a bad cold. So, it sounded more like, "Have a dice day." Remember? And you said, "Hello," right back. You didn't even look up. You were so shy. I'll never forget it.

EICHERSEN
    I don't—recall that.

JACKIE
    "Have a dice day."

EICHERSEN
    Well, it was very *dice* to meet you, Jackie. Now if you'll just—please—excuse me—I—

    The regular PATRON re-enters, sitting towards the back.

JACKIE
    Wait. I don't understand.

EICHERSEN
    What's to understand?

JACKIE
    Did I say something wrong? I didn't mean to say anything wrong. I just wanted to give you a complimentary hand job, and maybe some style pointers on your hair. Sorry, was that out of line? I used to be a hairdresser is all.

EICHERSEN
    No; I appreciate the styling advice.

JACKIE
    It's been a while since I cut anybody's hair.

EICHERSEN
    Is that—?

JACKIE
    Change of vocations. Not entirely my choice, but that's the way things go, right?

EICHERSEN
    Is it?

JACKIE
    I really wanted to be a paranormal psychologist, but I guess a person doesn't really have that many choices in their life.

EICHERSEN
None, really.

JACKIE
That's the whole tragic tale.

EICHERSEN
I get the ... It's been a downward trajectory.

JACKIE
Trajectory, is that it? I really like that word. Can I ask you something?

EICHERSEN
No.

JACKIE
Terence says you gave him a hundred dollars.

EICHERSEN
Oh, I see. That's what this is.

JACKIE
What? You think I'm asking for money?

EICHERSEN
No?

JACKIE
I'm not asking for money.

EICHERSEN
Oh, I get it. Asking for it by not asking for it.

JACKIE
Huh?

EICHERSEN
Offering your—"complimentary services." And then—and then—expecting something in return, I suppose. Well, I'm one step ahead of you, Jackie. I'll give you fifty dollars to go away.

JACKIE
He said you would say something like that.

EICHERSEN
    Who?

JACKIE
    Lomy.

EICHERSEN
    Lomy doesn't know me. Lomy is—

JACKIE
    You're wrong. Lomy knows people.

    The PATRON moves a little closer.

    He studies them like a science. Not individually, as a rule, but as a social phenomenon.
    (*to the PATRON*) Hi.

EICHERSEN
    He killed my girlfriend's dog. Did you know that?

JACKIE
    Why would he do something like that?

EICHERSEN
    Because he somehow got the impression that I didn't like the thing.

JACKIE
    Maybe you've inspired him.

EICHERSEN
    To kill a dog.

JACKIE
    He says you changed his life.

EICHERSEN
    Well, I had no intention of—I had no intention. The hundred dollars was—

JACKIE
    Did you do it for him or for you?

EICHERSEN
    Which answer is going to least impress you?

JACKIE
You're so humble.

EICHERSEN
I'm not.

JACKIE
That's a good sign. I think really good people in this world are the ones who never boast about it. Not like Archie. Archie is all, "Oh, I killed that guy with one hand," or whatever.

EICHERSEN
One hand?

JACKIE
You're so adorable. I like the way you worry. Look at those wrinkles. Hey, I like your skin.

EICHERSEN
Why?

JACKIE
You could never ever hurt anybody.

EICHERSEN
I think I could. If I—if I—

JACKIE
Look at this.

She shows bruising on her leg.

EICHERSEN
What's that?

JACKIE
Could you do that? Fucking men. Fucking, *fucking* men.

EICHERSEN
I'm a man.

JACKIE
Well, you are and you aren't, if you get what I'm saying.

EICHERSEN
No, I—

JACKIE
I mean, just because you have a dick, doesn't mean you have to act like one.

EICHERSEN
I can be, I can be quite—dicky. Just the other day I was in the elevator—

JACKIE
Yeah?

EICHERSEN
What are you doing? Don't do that. Yes, and, and the door was closing and there was this old woman with a walker and I thought, "I don't want to share this elevator with an old woman," so I, so I—what are you doing?

JACKIE
I just want to be close to you.

EICHERSEN
No, you don't.

JACKIE
Just for a little.

EICHERSEN
Is this—? I have a girlfriend.

JACKIE
I need someone to be kind to me. Just for a little bit. Hold me.

EICHERSEN
I—

He finds himself holding onto JACKIE; a beat of silence. The PATRON moves closer.

Is that—enough?

JACKIE
Just hold me, for fuck's sake.

She starts to cry.

EICHERSEN
Don't ... Why are you crying?

JACKIE
Sorry.

EICHERSEN
Look, I don't know what the story is, here, but this is—

JACKIE
I hate my life.

EICHERSEN
Well, we all hate our lives. There's nothing new in that. (*to the PATRON*) Do you mind, sir?

JACKIE
You hate your life, too?

EICHERSEN
I didn't say that.

JACKIE
Yes, you did.

EICHERSEN
Well, yes I hate my life. I don't hate my life. My life is ... What I meant was—life isn't something you enjoy, necessarily. It's something you tolerate as best you can. My God, I'm sure even the Queen of England hates her life, on some level.

JACKIE
Really?

EICHERSEN
Look at all the stupid things she has to do. And those hats.

JACKIE
She doesn't have to stand on the corner, making moves.

EICHERSEN
She's stuck on her own particular corner. And she has to make a lot of moves.

JACKIE
> Does she have to have sex with ugly old johns?

EICHERSEN
> Just the one.

JACKIE
> Are you saying the Queen is a whore?

EICHERSEN
> I'm saying we're all whores, Jackie. And we all have pimps, only mine, for example, happens to be an orthotic shoe sales manager.

JACKIE
> Really?

EICHERSEN
> Really.

JACKIE
> You see, you're so good, Ozzie.

EICHERSEN
> I'm not good. Why am I good?

JACKIE
> You treat a woman with respect; you can talk to a woman.

EICHERSEN
> I can't talk to my girlfriend.

JACKIE
> Why not?

EICHERSEN
> Because she's cold and untouchable. Because she always thinks I've got only one thing on my mind. And I do; only I can't let her know that, so I act like it's not on my mind at all.

JACKIE
> Poor Ozzie.

EICHERSEN
> Oh. *Oh*. My. As techniques goes, that's—

JACKIE
>I learned it in my pottery class.

>>*EICHERSEN begins to make a lot of strange noises. The PATRON hunches down in his seat, making more noises. AUDREY enters, tentatively, looking about, stopping at the PATRON, to inhale her disgust. Walks down the aisle, discovering EICHERSEN "in flagrante delicto."*

AUDREY
>Oswald!

JACKIE
>Hi.

EICHERSEN
>Audrey! What, what are you doing here?

AUDREY
>You asked me to come. What is going on?

EICHERSEN
>This is—this is—

JACKIE
>Jackie DaSousa.

AUDREY
>I really don't care. Oswald—

EICHERSEN
>I can explain.

JACKIE
>If this is awkward, I can come back and finish later.

AUDREY
>No. Carry on—please.

EICHERSEN
>Don't carry on. Stop. Audrey, listen—

JACKIE
>Excuse me.

>>*JACKIE makes her way out of her seat and past AUDREY.*

>I'll see you later.

AUDREY
>   Oh, will you?

EICHERSEN
>   Don't be like that, Audrey.

JACKIE
>   Yeah, don't be like that.

AUDREY
>   Like what?

EICHERSEN
>   I don't know, like a cliché of an injured party. She means well.

AUDREY
>   I can see that.

JACKIE
>   Can I have that fifty dollars now?

EICHERSEN
>   I can explain all this. Just—sit down for a minute. Here.

>   *He gives her some money.*

>   Go.

JACKIE
>   See you later.

EICHERSEN
>   No.

>   *She goes.*

>   She won't—see me later. Don't look like that.

AUDREY
>   Like a cliché, you mean.

EICHERSEN
>   Sit down.

AUDREY
>   Here?

EICHERSEN
Audrey—please.

She moves down the row, and sits.

AUDREY
This is not where I see us going in our relationship.

EICHERSEN
Me, neither.

AUDREY
I thought things were going so well. Even Dr. Strauss said—

EICHERSEN
They are, presently.

AUDREY
You don't mean "presently," you mean "at present." What is that man doing?

EICHERSEN
I don't know.

(*to the* PATRON) Excuse me, but we're having a private conversation.

The PATRON gets up and moves to the back. They all sit in silence. AUDREY turns and looks at EICHERSEN.

AUDREY
Ozzie—

EICHERSEN
There you go, jumping to conclusions.

AUDREY
Well, have you lost your mind?

EICHERSEN
I don't know.

AUDREY
Why did you kill Rebecca?

EICHERSEN
I did not—OK, can I just say that, first of all, you should never have given that dog a human name—

AUDREY
It isn't a human name, it's a Daphne du Maurier character.

EICHERSEN
Alright, let's just try to stick to the point.

AUDREY
Oh, there's a point—oh, good. There's a point.

EICHERSEN
I did not kill your dog.

AUDREY
No? You left a note.

EICHERSEN
That's—it wasn't me, Audrey. Do you think I would ever be able to do that? Even if I wanted to?

AUDREY
Why would you want to?

EICHERSEN
That's exactly what I'm saying. You know how squeamish I am. Listen to me; I know who did it.

AUDREY
What are my feet sticking to?

EICHERSEN
Are you listening to me? There's this guy, Audrey. His name is Lomy. He's a street person. I gave him a hundred dollars.

AUDREY
To kill Rebecca?

EICHERSEN
Of course not. That, he did as a kind of—courtesy. He thought he was doing me a favour.

AUDREY
How would that be a favour?

EICHERSEN
Well, he got it into his head that I didn't like—Rebecca. Somehow he got the idea that I hated her because she, in some small, growling, sharp-toothed little way, represented, you know, some aspect of—I don't know—you.

AUDREY
What gave him that idea?

EICHERSEN
Well, for one thing, he's crazy. Did I mention that?

AUDREY
I don't get this. Why did you give a crazy street person a hundred dollars?

EICHERSEN
Oh, Audrey. I don't know. You know how, in your life, one or two times in your life, you do something completely inconsistent? Well, I know you never have, but you truly are an exception.

AUDREY
I should hope so.

EICHERSEN
See? That's—that's ... The thing is, I'd just gone to the ATM. I had a hundred dollars in my pocket. I can't even explain it to myself. I looked at him, standing there, with that dirty little box of his, and I expected him to ask me for change, because he always asks me for change, whenever I go into the building or come out of the building. But this time he didn't. He just looked at me, and then turned away. Didn't ask for anything. As if he was saying, "Oh, it's you; you won't give me anything, you never give me anything because that's the kind of person you are." And I thought, "Oh, yeah? You think I'm predictable? Well, fuck you, then. Here!" Is that—? Is that—?

AUDREY

If you become insane, I won't know what to do.

EICHERSEN

Insane? I'm not insane. It's this—Lomy guy.

AUDREY

It's not that I don't have sympathy for crazy people. I have sympathy for crazy people. What was that movie, the one where they were all running around with cricket bats? There were midgets who couldn't get up on the beds. It was German.

EICHERSEN

It would pretty much have to be.

AUDREY

And who is this woman? This woman with her hands down your pants?

EICHERSEN

Well, that's Jackie. A friend of this Lomy guy. He got it into his head that I needed to have sex with her.

AUDREY

Oswald. I hate to ask, because you seem so convinced, but does this guy really exist? I mean—

EICHERSEN

What?

AUDREY

What does this guy look like? This Lomy guy—

EICHERSEN

I'm not making him up.

AUDREY

So, what does he look like? Does he look like you?

EICHERSEN

Nothing like me.

AUDREY
Of course. You see? He's your nemesis. You invent this guy so that you can do things that you wouldn't normally do, because you don't have the—what are those things called?

EICHERSEN
Balls?

AUDREY
Instincts. Remember when you tried to kill that mouse with the insect spray? So, a dog—you see what I mean?

EICHERSEN
No.

AUDREY
You would have to invent a whole new personality in order to kill a dog that you loved.

EICHERSEN
What are you saying?

AUDREY
Not to mention having sex with a prostitute in a porn theatre.

EICHERSEN
Let's clear a few things up here, Audrey. First of all, they sometimes show art films in here. Second, I did not kill your fucking little dog.

AUDREY
Oswald. That word.

EICHERSEN
And secondly—

AUDREY
You've done secondly.

EICHERSEN
OK, lastly, then: I was not having sex with a prostitute. Yes, she is a prostitute, but she was a hairdresser who had every intention of becoming a paranormal

psychologist, and it was her who was having sex with me. And it wasn't sex, it was a hand job.

AUDREY
This is the internet, isn't it? You've been looking at pictures again.

EICHERSEN
I was shopping for underwear.

AUDREY
Women's underwear?

EICHERSEN
For you.

AUDREY
That's another thing. Why have you become so obsessed with sex, lately?

EICHERSEN
You think I'm obsessed with sex?

AUDREY
You've brought it up three times this past month.

EICHERSEN
Did I?

AUDREY
You know my position on penises.

EICHERSEN
I didn't know you had one.

AUDREY
I just—I find them—one-dimensional.

EICHERSEN
What if I am going insane?

AUDREY
You need to talk to Dr. Strauss.

EICHERSEN
But, how could I imagine him? He has a pink bow on one side of his head. You know how symmetrical I am.

AUDREY
Can we please get out of here?

EICHERSEN
Wait.

AUDREY
What?

EICHERSEN
Go down on me.

AUDREY
What?

EICHERSEN
There's no one around. It'll be an adventure.

AUDREY
I'm not listening to any more of this. I'm going. I'm—what is happening to you?

EICHERSEN
Don't you ever crave adventure, for God's sake?

AUDREY
No. And neither do you. Adventure?

EICHERSEN
Audrey.

AUDREY
You killed my dog.

EICHERSEN
Stay and watch the second feature with me.

AUDREY
This is—insane.

She goes as the lights dim and the film begins.

EICHERSEN
    Audrey!

> *He turns back, thinks for a moment.*

It is. It's insane. It's—absolutely ...

> *He looks up at the screen, watches, then slinks down into his seat. The PATRON makes his way down the aisle and sits across from EICHERSEN.*
>
> *Blackout.*

Scene Three

Another day. The film is running, but then we see numbers and a blank screen; the theatre is empty. EICHERSEN enters, and sits.

The film starts up again. In a moment, LOMY enters. He sits well behind EICHERSEN, unnoticed by him; they both watch for a bit. EICHERSEN is agitated, and looks about, finally noticing somebody at the back.

EICHERSEN
Lomy?

LOMY
Yeah?

EICHERSEN
Is that you?

LOMY
Who? Are you talking to me?

EICHERSEN
Lomy?

LOMY
You talking to me?

EICHERSEN
You'd better tell me what's going on, Lomy. Right now. What is going on?

LOMY
I think she's applying for a job with the airline; but she has to take her top off first.

EICHERSEN
You know what I'm talking about. What's this about bullet holes?

LOMY
Beats me. Bullet holes?

EICHERSEN
Somebody put two bullet holes in my psychiatrist's car. Left a note.

LOMY gets up from his seat and comes down to join EICHERSEN.

LOMY
Somebody shot at your shrink's car and left a note? Now that's scary.

EICHERSEN
Yes, it is.

LOMY
I can't say I'm surprised, though.

EICHERSEN
No?

LOMY
The guy is a fucking criminal.

EICHERSEN
Is that right.

LOMY
Yeah, he robs you of your whole personality.

EICHERSEN
That's his job.

LOMY
He is standing in the way of your happiness, man.

EICHERSEN
And how does he do that, exactly?

LOMY
> Do you want to get into this? OK. Let's get into this. There is nothing wrong with you. It's all psychological.

EICHERSEN
> Well, of course it is.

LOMY
> Someone's gotta be on the lookout for my buddy, here.

EICHERSEN
> What are—? Why are you doing this?

LOMY
> I find that question kind of pathetic, Oswald, and a little irritating. You know why I am doing this; I told you why. You have reignited my interest in humanity. You have given my life a centrifugal force.

EICHERSEN
> Oh, terrific.

LOMY
> I never had that.

EICHERSEN
> I don't want to be the centrifugal force in yours or anybody's life. It requires gravity. I don't have any gravity. See?

LOMY
> You have gravity.

EICHERSEN
> Stop touching me.

LOMY
> I'm not ashamed of my feelings.

EICHERSEN
> I am.

LOMY
> This guy, this shrink, has convinced you that you aren't happy, see?

EICHERSEN
   I'm not.

LOMY
   Exactly. But you are. You are happy—underneath all that unhappiness. This criminal, this scam artist, has made you doubt your own feelings.

EICHERSEN
   Is that why you shot at his car?

LOMY
   It wasn't me.

EICHERSEN
   Oh, it wasn't.

LOMY
   But the scales are tipping. They're tipping.

EICHERSEN
   What's wrong with you? You look—

LOMY
   It's nothing. Medication.

EICHERSEN
   And where did you get a gun, by the way—and what medication?

LOMY
   A gun?

EICHERSEN
   A gun.

LOMY
   Is that what you want to talk about? Let's talk about us, about what's happening here.

EICHERSEN
   Alright. Why are you ruining my life?

LOMY
   I'm ruining your life, and you're dating a woman who sells commercial real estate and won't even blow you?

EICHERSEN
    You have my credit card, and my driver's license. You think I wouldn't notice?

LOMY
    I don't have them.

EICHERSEN
    Of course you do.

LOMY
    Why don't you just go to the police, man?

EICHERSEN
    Because the police are not going to believe me. Why would a street person, that I don't even know, shoot at my psychiatrist's car? Murder my girlfriend's dog? Write angry, life-threatening letters to my mother? Does that make sense to you?

LOMY
    Does anything make sense? How do you suppose I feel in all this? I don't like doing bad things any more than you do.

EICHERSEN
    Then stop. Get out of my life.

LOMY
    You talk about it like it's a thing that already happened. "My Life." Like the book is written and the film is already out. *Man*. Look at you: all wild-eyed. I just ... You are so—caught up in all this.

EICHERSEN
    Don't.

LOMY
    Your life is still happening. It's changing every minute. What is a life? What is it? Tell me what it is.

EICHERSEN
    Well, clearly something you don't have.

LOMY
>Don't say things you'll later regret. OK? And, OK, I would have had to agree with you, two weeks ago. But I know different, now. A life is a thing we know nothing about. We think we know, but we don't. I was standing there, thinking it was going one way, and then you came along and took it in another direction. Like the biblical, you know, "through a glass, darkly." You know?

EICHERSEN
>No, I don't know.

LOMY
>Through a glass, darkly. This is hard, man. This is hard for us. New territory. I think I need you to put your arm around my shoulder.

EICHERSEN
>No, thank you.

LOMY
>Put your arm around my shoulder.
>
>>*He does.*
>
>I'm scared, Ozzie. Suddenly I'm thinking, "What if this all turns out badly? What if somebody gets hurt?"

EICHERSEN
>What do you want?

LOMY
>Here's some back-story. I fought in a war, Oswald. Did I ever tell you that?

EICHERSEN
>No.

LOMY
>In all this time, I've never told you. Wow. Yeah, I fought in a war of avarice, disguised as a war for good. I put my life on the line. Why? I mean, I was paid, sure, but you don't crawl through jungles to kill people because you're paid. You believe; on some level, you believe. You don't walk into a town in the middle of nowhere and start

popping women and children without a purpose in mi. The other side is bad. I don't know why, exactly. It's Africa; some—I don't know … What the fuck do I know about Africa? What does anybody know—or care?

EICHERSEN
I care.

LOMY
Do you? Do you?

EICHERSEN
I have been—known to care.

LOMY
I was fighting for the good side. That's what I was, you know, fighting for. I kick over this metal siding. There's a girl lying dead, with a little Bible in her hand, flies all over her. Little pink ribbon in her hair. I don't know if it was me who shot her. Somebody did. A little white Bible. In her little hand. I took it; pried it from her little hand.

His tone shifts.

You know, once you divest yourself of purpose, killing just becomes an exercise in accuracy; it's target practice. I never even read the paper after I came back. I don't even know which side won. Maybe they're still fighting. But I couldn't do it anymore. I lost my fear. When you don't have fear, you can't do it anymore. Fear is what keeps it real. I lost my fear.

EICHERSEN
Is that—right.

LOMY
I was—yeah—on a beach somewhere, yeah. I think I was going to shoot myself in the head. An angel came to me; I know this sounds crazy, but an angel appeared to me, except it really looked more like a little man with really separated teeth, and he looked up at me and he said, "Terence, do not shoot yourself. Here is a stone—this is your soul; keep this with you always."

EICHERSEN
   He had quite a—high-pitched voice.

LOMY
   He was just a little guy.

EICHERSEN
   Did he have wings?

LOMY
   Wings are not what angels are about.

EICHERSEN
   OK. I didn't—now I know.

LOMY
   I gave him everything I had, and took the stone. I *relinquished* my life to him. Wasn't much. My wallet, my watch, my clothes.

EICHERSEN
   Clothes?

LOMY
   Funny, we see our life. It's right there in front of us. Like this movie here: a story, unfolding.

EICHERSEN
   Story?

LOMY
   Yeah. What? Yeah. We see this picture, here, but if we were on the other side of that screen, there, we'd be looking at exactly the opposite thing. It would look like the same thing, except it would be the opposite. You know what I mean? The picture would be flipped. You know what I'm saying?

EICHERSEN
   No.

LOMY
   You do. You know. You just don't want to admit it. You're so funny, sometimes. I just have to laugh.

EICHERSEN
> No, I really don't have any idea what you're talking about. Africa, movie screens, angels with bad teeth; there doesn't seem to be a central point to any of this.

LOMY
> You're so *focused. Man.* You are—wow.

EICHERSEN
> Could I—not—put my arm around you now?

LOMY
> Yeah, I feel better. But, hey, buddy, what about you in all this? I worry about you in all this.
>
> You're moving way outside the normal parameters of your life; that's gotta be tough.

EICHERSEN
> But I don't want to move outside the parameters. I prefer to stay well within. Within.

LOMY
> What the future is, is unknown.

EICHERSEN
> I realize that.

LOMY
> You don't realize that. You have it all mapped out in your fucking head. But, hey, wait a second; it doesn't make any sense, this *thing* you got ahead of you, so you go see your shrink, so it'll make fucking sense. So he can fit you into a box and FedEx you to your final destination.

EICHERSEN
> Why did you break into my apartment?

LOMY
> Because you inspired me, Oswald. You gave me a hundred dollars, and that was more than enough payment for the work ahead.

EICHERSEN
> There is no work ahead. What work ahead?

LOMY
>   Don't ask so many questions. I really don't have the answers; I don't. I just know it's going to be great for you, now that you have opened the door up to a different future.

EICHERSEN
>   Let's close it. Let's just close that door.

LOMY
>   We can't. You robbed a bank an hour ago.

EICHERSEN
>   I did?

LOMY
>   Isn't that exciting? But, hey, you know what?

EICHERSEN
>   A bank?

LOMY
>   You dropped your ID on the way out. Life, eh?

EICHERSEN
>   ID?

LOMY
>   Yikes!

EICHERSEN
>   You, you, you—

LOMY
>   Isn't it just crazy what happens when you flip things around? Look.
>
>   *Handing EICHERSEN a fistful of money.*
>
>   I know. It's so fucked. Hey, don't worry about all the cash. You look so worried. Don't worry.

EICHERSEN
>   No?

LOMY
>   We can launder it on the street with—you know.

EICHERSEN
   No, I—

LOMY
   I got a guy. We just have to be careful who we sell our drugs back to, that's all.

EICHERSEN
   Drugs?

LOMY
   Isn't it just nuts? What a fucking roller coaster. Do you believe in God, Oswald? Do you?

EICHERSEN
   God?

LOMY
   Exactly—neither do I; so you see? You see? We've got all this good work to do, all on our own. But, hey, that's OK. If we don't do it, who the fuck will?

   Beat. He watches the film, as EICHERSEN counts the money.

   Look at that. I guess she got the job.

   He passes out. EICHERSEN continues to watch as the lights fade; police sirens in the distance.
   Blackout.
   Interval.

Scene Four

Movie theatre. No film. LOMY is asleep, wakes with a start. AUDREY enters. She walks tentatively down the aisle. Sits. LOMY watches her, then approaches and sits behind her, off to one side.

LOMY
    Hi.

AUDREY
    Oh. My.

LOMY
    I hope I didn't frighten you. Sorry.

AUDREY
    I'm meeting someone; thank you.

LOMY
    You're meeting me.

AUDREY
    I'm sorry; I am not meeting you. I don't know where you got that impression.

LOMY
    It's not an impression. It's a fact. Oswald can't be here. I apologize for that.

AUDREY
    What?

LOMY
    I said, "Oswald cannot be here and I apologize for that." But, for obvious reasons, he cannot make an appearance. The police are after him, at the moment.

AUDREY
    I know.

LOMY
    Oh, so you know.

AUDREY
    He's wanted for questioning in connection with a bank robbery.

LOMY
    This is a euphemism they use. They need to locate him so that they can arrest him. He can't tell you where he is at the moment. He's sorry about that, but that's just the way it is.

AUDREY
    Why did he ask me to come down here, if he doesn't want me to know where he is?

LOMY
    He needs to get some stuff out in the open. He's got some stuff, some issues, OK? With you.

AUDREY
    Obviously. He killed my dog and blamed it on a, on a street person. Are you this guy he talks about?

LOMY
    I don't think so.

AUDREY
    Oh.

LOMY
    Alright, I am.

AUDREY
    I see. Did you kill my dog?

LOMY
    I wish I could own up to that, you know; but I really think that Oswald needs to take more responsibility for his actions. You smell especially nice.

AUDREY
> Thank you.

LOMY
> I hope that doesn't embarrass you. Like a sweet cucumber, almost. Is that—Givenchy?

AUDREY
> No.

LOMY
> One of the benefits of not doing anything all day is that you get to familiarize yourself with the different scents in the cosmetic sections of all the various drug stores—throughout our city.

AUDREY
> Lovely.

LOMY
> It is lovely. It's a chance to imagine what a woman might smell like, lying next to you. It's been a while. I'm sorry; that was inappropriate. That was—

AUDREY
> Yes, it was.

LOMY
> So, I hear you're in commercial real estate. That's a very sexy line of work.

AUDREY
> What are these "issues" he has with me, exactly?

LOMY
> Well, I'm not privy to the inner workings of his mind, Miss, but from what I can tell, he thinks you're "kind of hot" but "a little uptight." I think those are the words he used. If only you'd let your hair down a little. Here.

AUDREY
> Please.

LOMY
> You should play with the volume a little.

AUDREY
I am not uptight in the least.

LOMY
Sure, OK. Let's discuss it.

AUDREY
I don't want to discuss it.

LOMY
I understand. Sure.

AUDREY
Has it occurred to him *at all* that women have different needs from men, I wonder. Has that occurred to him?

LOMY
I think he's aware of that. I think most of us are aware of that.

AUDREY
Uptight. That's such a—such an easy thing to say.

LOMY
It is.

AUDREY
It nicely, neatly uncomplicates things, doesn't it?

LOMY
I'm not sure that's a verb, exactly; however, yes, you're right. It's an easy thing to say. But, sometimes, it's right to uncomplicate things. I'll give you an example, if I may. Pardon my breath; I have a rotting tooth that at some point may have to be looked at.

AUDREY
That's—fine.

LOMY
A couple of guys kicked the shit out of me, once. Did I ever tell you this story? We got a lot of catching up to do.

AUDREY
Please—don't—touch my hair.

Couple of guys in the military, which I found
.ppointing, as you can imagine, having been a soldier
.yself for a couple of years there. They dragged me into
an alley, yeah, and kicked the fucking daylights out of
me. The blood was so thick around my eyes—I'm sorry,
my language—so thick around my eyes that it dried
before I regained consciousness. So, when I woke up, I
thought I'd gone blind. Right? I lay there for the longest
time, trying to reorganize my life, in my head, anyways.
Trying to think how I would manage without my sight,
you know? Just the daily ins and outs of it. How do I go
to the bathroom, for instance; I don't mean the crapping
part, but wiping my ass. We may not like to talk about it,
but proper and complete ass-wiping is an extremely
important part of the personal hygiene package. You want
to make sure—

AUDREY
I think I—get the picture.

LOMY
Sure. You're an intelligent woman: a very attractive, very
intelligent woman. You understand that blindness,
especially for a down-and-out asshole like me, is critical
in my business, and I call it a business when in fact it's
anything but. Well, I suppose it is, if you think of it as
part of the overall economic strategy. In my business you
have to keep a watchful eye: on yourself, on your
belongings. It's not like a security company is coming
around to check on your stuff. How does one keep a
watchful eye when they're blind? In the end, of course—
and I don't even know if there's a moral to this story—in
the end, my sight came back. But, by then, I had so
complicated things in my mind with the whole idea of
blindness, that my life suddenly seemed, now—seemed to
me, at any rate—a fairly simple one. I was a worthless
piece of shit; but at least I could see that. It was
liberating—in a kind of painful, blood-encrusted way.

AUDREY
   Well, that's—wonderful.

LOMY
   It is?

AUDREY
   That you didn't go blind.

LOMY
   Yeah, I saw one of those boys a couple of weeks later. Drunk, in the same alley. Oh, I remember the moral, now. I murdered him. I didn't actually murder him. Well, yes I did. I did, I suppose. I put him in the dumpster, and he got crushed the next morning. It was—yeah. It pretty much uncomplicated things for me. I know it doesn't quite qualify as fate, exactly. I had a hand in it, but ... But anyway, those days are over. I don't seek revenge, now. Oswald has inspired me to do good.

AUDREY
   Oswald?

LOMY
   He has taken a person without hope, without caring, without anything but contempt and a blanket, and some lemon loaf he didn't really want, and lifted him up, up.

AUDREY
   And how has he done that?

LOMY
   Because he showed me something that no one has ever shown me. I don't mean generosity. He has shown me need.

AUDREY
   Is that his jacket?

LOMY
   This?

AUDREY
   That's his jacket you have on.

LOMY
> See what I mean? His own jacket. I can't believe how well it fits me.

AUDREY
> Have you done something with him?

LOMY
> Audrey—may I call you Audrey?

AUDREY
> No.

LOMY
> Audrey, I haven't done anything to him. He's done something to himself. He has made himself into a new person. Well, not entirely—not yet. He's still in the process.

AUDREY
> I see; so robbing a bank is part of this process?

> *The regular PATRON enters and takes a seat at the back.*

LOMY
> That was just a divestment, was what that was. A putting aside, once and for all, Audrey, of these tired old dreams of his, you know? This—lame ambition. How else can I describe it? The guy sells orthopedic shoes.

AUDREY
> Someone has to.

LOMY
> This was really more of a statement than a bank robbery. It was a calling out for change. Change! What's happening is nothing short of amazing.

> *The PATRON dons a surgical mask.*

AUDREY
> So—is part of this change disowning his own mother?

LOMY
> He did that?

AUDREY
>   He mailed her a small parcel of feces.
>
>   *A noise.*
>
>   What was that?

LOMY
>   A box of shit—gee, I'm impressed.

AUDREY
>   You are.

LOMY
>   It shows a kind of maturity. It's a link to the past. The past, Audrey, is not the future. We don't know what the future is. It's something we determine, every day. You could change, too. You could free yourself from the slavery of your—life right now.

AUDREY
>   It's hardly slavery. What is that man doing?

LOMY
>   Look at you.

AUDREY
>   What's wrong with me?

LOMY
>   Are you kidding me? You're kidding me. Here, let me give you a neck rub. Just—forget about him.

AUDREY
>   I don't want a neck rub. Get away from me.

LOMY
>   You see? You can't let go. What are you afraid of?

AUDREY
>   You, for one thing.

LOMY
>   You people, you know. You just—you have all the opportunity in the world. You have minds, and healthy bodies, and a decent environment, a nice clean place to

live, and all this education and imagination and what do you do? You make a cage for yourself and you lock yourself in it. That is a very flattering colour on you, I have to say: a very flattering colour. Look, may I remove that?

AUDREY
Certainly—not. You may not.

LOMY
You're hanging onto things, Audrey.

AUDREY
Like my top, you mean?

LOMY
That's just one of many things. It's a symbol. It's a—you know? It's an idea. That's all. Let's uncomplicate it.

The PATRON moves closer.

AUDREY
It's a little more than an idea. It's all that stands between me and indecent exposure.

LOMY
What? You're not wearing a bra?

AUDREY
Yes, I'm wearing a bra.

LOMY
Exactly. Look. Oswald is on the verge of becoming a new person. And unless you're willing to become a new person, too, I don't think he's interested. I mean, that's the vibe I'm getting.

AUDREY
I can't, I'm sorry, I can't see how taking my top off in a porn theatre makes me a new person. And I don't see how it symbolizes anything—except a dirty mind.

(*to the PATRON*) Can I help you?

LOMY
(*also to the PATRON*) Buddy, we're having a rendezvous here.

AUDREY
We're not having a rendezvous.

The PATRON gets up and moves back a few rows.

LOMY
You think sex is dirty. This is your problem. This is the whole thing, right there.

AUDREY
Look, I don't know who you are, or what your story is, but if you are facilitating some sort of acting out on his part, I want you to stop. He is a modest person. He is compliant with the law, and quite unassuming. He has never in his life had so much as an unpaid parking ticket.

LOMY
Let me ask you something. Does he pay the parking ticket because he thinks he should or because it's owed?

AUDREY
He does what he's supposed to. Is that man masturbating?

LOMY
And this is what you love about him?

AUDREY
Who?

LOMY
Oswald.

AUDREY
It's what I find reassuring.

LOMY
OK. I get it. So, what is it you love about him?

AUDREY
Love about him?

LOMY
   Is that a—is that an impertinent question?

AUDREY
   I need to get out of here.

LOMY
   If he only does what he's supposed to in life, then maybe he just loves you because he's supposed to—because it's owed, if you know what I'm saying. You know what I'm saying. Doesn't sound to me like he makes a lot of real decisions. But, hey—Audrey—he gave me a hundred dollars.

AUDREY
   I heard.

LOMY
   Now *that* was a decision.

AUDREY
   He's never made a decision in his life.

   She gets up to go.

LOMY
   I think this was a great discussion, don't you? I mean—

AUDREY
   Was it?

LOMY
   Yeah; I think we got stuff out in the open here.

AUDREY
   Well, somebody certainly has. Look. Whatever you've done to Oswald, I want you to undo it.

LOMY
   It's not up to me. Oswald has a mind of his own, Audrey. Anyway, Jackie's taking good care of him, so don't worry about his physical needs. Maybe you should worry about your own.

AUDREY
Tell him from me that, when he's through thinking for himself, and taking care of his physical needs, when he's through exploring his options and making decisions, whatever those may be—

LOMY
Sure, I get you.

AUDREY
Tell him, tell him, he knows where to find me.

LOMY
Wouldn't it be great if he didn't know where to find you for a change? Know what I'm saying?

A beat.

Sure. I'll tell him.

She goes up the aisle, stopping for a beat at the row with the PATRON; suddenly, she slaps his face.

AUDREY
This is a heritage building!

She goes. After a moment, the disembodied voice of EICHERSEN just behind LOMY.

EICHERSEN
Is she gone?

LOMY
Hey, Oswald. I just had an idea.

EICHERSEN appears.

EICHERSEN
You mailed my mother a box of feces?

LOMY
Hey, I was thinking. You ought to grow a beard. That would be—yeah.

EICHERSEN
Why didn't I say something?

LOMY
She would have gone straight to the police.

EICHERSEN
Am I completely lacking in moral character?

LOMY
What would you have said?

EICHERSEN
Please tell me what you're doing. Why is this happening?

LOMY
I am getting tired of my motives being questioned, man. Once and for all, and this has got to be the last time I go over this, I am stripping away all this shit from your life so that, at least, you can move forward into an indeterminate future.

EICHERSEN
There is nothing very reassuring about an indeterminate future; I want you to know that.

LOMY
By the way, I read your screenplay.

EICHERSEN
You—you ... That is—that is none of your business.

LOMY
Oh, I think it is. I think stilted dialogue and awkward scene structure is very much my business. Hey, buddy, no worries. I fixed it.

A beat of EICHERSEN fuming.

Look at you!

EICHERSEN
Lomy, I know you think you're doing good for me; I'm convinced of that, now. I see, now, that—yes—you're completely—I don't know if this is technically the correct word, but *insane*, and—

LOMY
> Are you going to get all focused, now? Is this going to be a focused thing?

EICHERSEN
> *And*—if I may finish—

LOMY
> *And*, sure. *And*.

EICHERSEN
> And there is nothing wrong with insanity; one might even argue that it offers you a certain unique perspective, but, has it occurred to you—even momentarily, just in some weird flash of unexpected, I don't know, clarity, lucidity, common sense—that what you consider good for me might actually be, for lack of a better word, bad?

LOMY
> Of course you're going to think that. That is classic. Have you even been addicted to heroin?

EICHERSEN
> Let's see: No.

LOMY
> Or, well, addicted to anything, really; pick your substance. Something. You can't be that—

EICHERSEN
> Do we have to do this?

LOMY
> Yes.

EICHERSEN
> Peanuts. How's that?

LOMY
> Right, exactly, man. So, you lie to yourself.

EICHERSEN
> I do?

LOMY
    You say anything to get near to those peanuts again. You say, "I'll just put them over here for a second," knowing full well that you have to pass by them eventually, on your way to feed your goldfish, say.

    EICHERSEN suddenly remembers.

EICHERSEN
    My goldfish.

LOMY
    They've been taken care of.

EICHERSEN
    You've been back to my apartment?

LOMY
    Now and again.

EICHERSEN
    What do you mean "now and again"? Wait; what do you mean "taken care of"?

LOMY
    You are not a goldfish kind of person.

EICHERSEN
    No?

LOMY
    Not anymore.

    Beat of sadness from EICHERSEN.

They'll find their way through the sewage system—believe me, I know from experience. You can't have goldfish, Oswald. Goldfish symbolize your self-imprisonment. You want to be a fucking fish in a bowl? You need to be in a river, man, a river.

    Beat.

What were we talking about?

EICHERSEN
    Peanuts.

LOMY
> Really? I hate peanuts. Oh, yeah. So, here's the thing. You are addicted to your old life, see? You are addicted to slavery. It happens. You know, after the slaves were freed, some of them, anyway, didn't want to go. Did you know that? Because freedom, Oswald, is sometimes worse than the alternative. It takes a lot of—I don't know what it takes a lot of, but whatever that is, that thing—a lot of it, to make a new path for yourself each and every day. To not have a set time to wake up at, or a certain thing to do, or a place to go, or a routine to fall into. I want you to think about those fish, man. They are thinking for themselves, now. There are no more fucking circles, man. Fuck the past. Fuck circles.

EICHERSEN
> Is there anything so terribly wrong with circles, Lomy? The past is what gives us direction. We can't see where we're going, but we can see where we've been.

LOMY
> You know what; that was nicely said.

EICHERSEN
> It's sort of a cliché, really.

LOMY
> Is it?

EICHERSEN
> I *like* to know where I'm going.

LOMY
> I can't do anything with this. I'm trying to fix this.

EICHERSEN
> See; this is what I'm really concerned about. Don't get me wrong. I really appreciate it, this incredible generosity of spirit, but what exactly might "fixing this" further entail? So far, it's been pretty, well—pretty—I guess the word is "criminal," and/or has involved the killing of animals—some very small.

LOMY
A goldfish is not an animal; let's not get carried away.

EICHERSEN
And robbing a bank; what's that? Is that, is that—

LOMY
We need to clear away all this stuff.

EICHERSEN
How about I do it voluntarily?

LOMY
Hey, I just thought of a new name for you.

EICHERSEN
You talk about choices, but you give me none.

LOMY
Albert Pennyfarthing. What do you think?

EICHERSEN
Pennyfarthing.

LOMY
Yeah.

EICHERSEN
Is that—hyphenated, or—?

LOMY
I don't know. I just thought of it.

EICHERSEN
It's—

LOMY
What's wrong with it?

EICHERSEN
Nothing, in and of itself. It sort of lacks—I don't know—dynamism?

LOMY
There you go. You can't predetermine. What makes you think that dynamism will have anything to do with your life? That puts too much pressure on you, right from the

get-go. Albert Pennyfarthing doesn't demand anything of you. It says, "maybe."

EICHERSEN
OK. But why do I need a new name?

LOMY
Well, in the most immediate sense, because you robbed a Credit Union.

EICHERSEN
It wasn't even a bank?

LOMY
Same thing.

EICHERSEN
And please quit saying I robbed it.

LOMY
Aside from that, you want to completely separate yourself from any part of who you were, because you'll just fall back on the old habits.

EICHERSEN
Peanuts?

LOMY
More than peanuts. The General Direction of Oswald Eichersen. Albert's not going there. Albert's going in a whole other direction. Albert's going—

EICHERSEN
Where is Albert going?

LOMY
That is a—that's a lovely question.

EICHERSEN
Isn't it?

An arm around EICHERSEN.

LOMY
Where is Albert Pennyfarthing going? You know—I can see a whole world opening up here.

EICHERSEN
   Really, I don't—see that.

LOMY
   I see buildings burning.

EICHERSEN
   Buildings.

LOMY
   Burning. I see a conflagration, man. I see you setting a match to the whole world. How else do we build a new one?

EICHERSEN
   How else?

LOMY
   A world of decency and goodness and true equality—unless you burn this rotten stinking heap of fucking garbage down to the smouldering ground. Wow—that's—that's amazing. You are amazing.

EICHERSEN
   Amazing.

LOMY
   Relax your shoulders there.

   A film begins.

   Relax. You're amazing.

   LOMY slouches back to watch the film; EICHERSEN remains seated upright as the lights fade.

Scene Five

AUDREY is seated, watching a film; it's just coming to an end. In a moment, EICHERSEN pops up from behind a seat.

EICHERSEN
  Psst. Audrey.

AUDREY
  Oswald!

EICHERSEN approaches, sits beside her.

  What's going on? That message was so weird and confusing.

EICHERSEN
  Don't ever make an important call from a payphone in a Dim Sum restaurant.

AUDREY
  What are you doing?

EICHERSEN
  I need you to help me.

AUDREY
  Dim Sum?

EICHERSEN
  I have to somehow get rid of Lomy.

AUDREY
  Your street person?

EICHERSEN
  Where did you get that dress?

AUDREY
Have you been eating at all?

EICHERSEN
I think I'm going to have to kill him.

AUDREY
Who?

EICHERSEN
Terence Lomy.

AUDREY
Are you listening to yourself?

EICHERSEN
What else can I do?

AUDREY
Go to the police. Give yourself up.

EICHERSEN
I can't do that.

AUDREY
You have to.

EICHERSEN
I didn't do anything.

AUDREY
It doesn't matter. The truth is all that matters.

EICHERSEN
Truth? Last night I set fire to a real estate office.

AUDREY
You did?

EICHERSEN
I didn't. Albert *Pennyfarthing* did.

AUDREY
Who?

EICHERSEN
He's given me a new name.

AUDREY
Who?

EICHERSEN
He's turning me into a whole other person.

AUDREY
I think you should take some responsibility for your own actions.

EICHERSEN
These are not my actions.

AUDREY
Ozzie—

EICHERSEN
God only knows what other crimes he's planning to commit on my behalf. I have to stop him.

AUDREY
You can't murder him.

EICHERSEN
Why not? Why can't I?

AUDREY
Murder is not the answer to our social problems.

EICHERSEN
This is not a social problem; this is a very personal problem.

AUDREY
You said yourself he thinks he's doing you a favour.

EICHERSEN
Audrey, he wants to destroy the world in order to make it better.

AUDREY
What's wrong with making the world better?

EICHERSEN
I'm talking about his methodology, here.

AUDREY
OK, his methodology is a little off—

EICHERSEN
A little?

AUDREY
People's intentions are important.

EICHERSEN
What are you—?

AUDREY
OK, let me just say, right off the bat, you're not going to like this.

EICHERSEN
Like what?

AUDREY
I'm sleeping with him.

Beat.

EICHERSEN
Who?

AUDREY
Your guy.

EICHERSEN
What?

AUDREY
Don't take it the wrong way, Ozzie. It isn't sexual.

EICHERSEN
Lomy?

AUDREY
There is a, certainly, a—an erotic element to it, but that's not the centrepiece.

EICHERSEN
You're sleeping with Lomy?

AUDREY
You say it like it was—I know. It's insane. I would say he talked me into it, but that would be a lie. I mean, he did talk me into it, but only by taking away the consequences.

EICHERSEN
How? How did he do that?

AUDREY
You said yourself you're no longer the same person. And if you're not who you are anymore—well—

EICHERSEN
I am the same person.

AUDREY
Didn't you say you weren't the same person?

EICHERSEN
No.

AUDREY
Well, regardless—

EICHERSEN
Regardless?

AUDREY
A person needs to make their own choices. I made a choice.

EICHERSEN
When did this happen?

AUDREY
Does it really matter? Yesterday.

Beat.

Would it upset you if I said it was incredible?

EICHERSEN
Yesterday?

AUDREY
I never really got the sex thing before. I just thought it was a—an amalgamation of genitalia. But this has a context; you know?

EICHERSEN
Does it?

AUDREY
When I got to your place—I know this is crazy—

EICHERSEN
My place?

AUDREY
You told me to meet you there.

EICHERSEN
I did?

AUDREY
In your note.

EICHERSEN
Note?

AUDREY
There he was, in your bathrobe. It's astonishing how little like you he looks in it.

EICHERSEN
You've never seen me in my bathrobe.

AUDREY
Haven't I?

EICHERSEN
This is—

AUDREY
I know. I *know*. Demented. I nearly ran back out the door, I had every intention, but there was something incredibly overpowering, something—he said, "Get in here and close the door," and I did. I just—but it wasn't because he told me to. It wasn't like a male power thing, or like a vocal

thing. He drew something out of me: my own humanitarianess.

EICHERSEN
That's not a word.

AUDREY
A panhandler, Ozzie, is a person, a real person. You can see why I don't want you to kill him. He's opened me up to myself—to a kinder, more generous me. Oh, Ozzie, don't look like that. Things happen. We can't see what's ahead of us. Through a glass, darkly—you know?

EICHERSEN
Well, you've certainly changed your tune, Audrey. Two days ago—

AUDREY
I know. Two days ago; isn't it amazing how things can change so quickly and so completely? It's like one of those—what are they called?

EICHERSEN
Brain tumours?

AUDREY
What do you think of my eyeshadow?

EICHERSEN
So, I guess your position on penises has—evolved somewhat.

AUDREY
You don't want to start comparing penises; believe me. And anyway, this isn't some pissing contest. I want you to see the plus-side of this.

EICHERSEN
OK.

AUDREY
I have realized that I am not shut off from the world. I have needs. Isn't it ironic that a simple beggar should teach me that?

EICHERSEN
> I could have told you that.

AUDREY
> With words, Ozzie. Only with words.

EICHERSEN
> I wanted to have sex with you right in this very theatre.

AUDREY
> You think that's what I want?

EICHERSEN
> I don't know what you want.

AUDREY
> Neither do I. Isn't it exciting? I don't know how I'm feeling about the whole Grand Cayman thing.

EICHERSEN
> Grand Cayman?

AUDREY
> Well, apparently he has a lot of money to launder.

EICHERSEN
> This is—

AUDREY
> I know.

EICHERSEN
> Audrey, I need you to help me get out of this situation. I had to panhandle a quarter just to call you. Can't you see what he's doing? It's some kind of social re-proportioning. It's, it's—

AUDREY
> I think you're analyzing it too much.

EICHERSEN
> Am I?

AUDREY
> Your life is falling apart, and you've created some elaborate—story. He told me all about it. How you

insisted on giving him everything you own. Why are you mocking him like that?

EICHERSEN
I'm going insane.

AUDREY
You need to see Dr. Strauss.

EICHERSEN
How? I not only shot at his car, I torched his office, and somehow broke his collarbone.

AUDREY
You shouldn't have.

EICHERSEN
I didn't!

AUDREY
I know.

EICHERSEN
You don't know. Don't say you know, in that patronizing—wearing that eye make-up that, I'm sorry, makes you look like a vampire with a pollen reaction. Lomy has disowned me, and discredited me, and left me hiding out from the law, and why? Because of a simple kindness?

AUDREY
It wasn't a kindness.

EICHERSEN
What was it, then? I gave him a hundred dollars.

AUDREY
I have to go pack.

EICHERSEN
Where are you going? Wait. Where are you going?

AUDREY
I told you.

EICHERSEN
He's a thief and a criminal.

AUDREY
>Even if he is, you can't really be a good person in a bad world, Ozzie.

EICHERSEN
>Did he tell you that?

>*She rises.*

AUDREY
>Charity, by the way, is not about giving.

EICHERSEN
>No?

AUDREY
>It's about fulfilling needs. Needs, Ozzie.

EICHERSEN
>Speaking of which; can you spare me some cash? I haven't had a decent meal in a week.

AUDREY
>Poor Ozzie. I feel so sorry for you. I really do. But if I just hand you money, I'm not really helping you, am I?

EICHERSEN
>Yes.

>*She goes up the aisle.*

>Audrey. Audrey.

>*She passes the regular PATRON on his way in.*

AUDREY
>Excuse me.

EICHERSEN
>Audrey!

>*She exits.*

>What is happening?

>*He exits. Dejected, the PATRON sits, alone.*
>*Blackout.*

Scene Six

EICHERSEN, alone, sleeps. He wakes with a horrified start. He looks about; finds himself holding an empty gasoline container.

Blackout.

Scene Seven

A film in progress: "Do it, do it," and "Don't stop, don't stop." LOMY watches, amused; looks at his watch. He is dressed head to toe in EICHERSEN's clothes. Slowly, from behind, EICHERSEN rises up. For a moment, he stands above LOMY, contemplating murder perhaps, or whatever passes though the mind of a desperate orthotic-shoe salesman.

LOMY
> This watch of yours is crap, by the way. Where's the second hand?

EICHERSEN
> You had this planned all along.

LOMY
> Had what planned?

EICHERSEN
> This whole elaborate enterprise, Lomy.

LOMY
> I don't know what you're talking about.

EICHERSEN
> And may I just say for the record—you make it rather hard for a person to imagine ever giving a panhandler money again.

LOMY
> Why should you?

EICHERSEN
> I don't understand what it is you have against charity. So, before I kill you, maybe you could explain that one little thing.

LOMY
You're not going to kill me.

EICHERSEN
I mean, yes, it was a foolish thing of me to do, and maybe in some weird way that pissed you off, because—I don't know—you thought I was being uncharitable by giving you a hundred dollars.

LOMY
We are way past a hundred dollars at this point.

EICHERSEN
Oh, you are so right about that.

LOMY
As usual, you've got everything turned upside down.

EICHERSEN
You took Audrey.

LOMY
You never had Audrey. She's not a possession. She is her own person. A voluptuous, a sexual—

EICHERSEN
Yeah, I get it.

LOMY
And she's out of your life. Pretty soon she'll be out of mine, so don't worry about her. Audrey needed to be released from the bondage of her thinking, that's all. You two, you were all tied up in this fucking thing, this thing that ties people up.

EICHERSEN
It's called a relationship.

LOMY
Is that what it's called?

EICHERSEN
You're wearing that inside out, by the way.

LOMY
Huh?

EICHERSEN

    The shirt is inside out. My shirt. My jacket.

LOMY

    Will you forget about this. This is nothing but a costume, man. If you could just get outside your head for half a fucking second.

EICHERSEN

    I like my head. I liked my goldfish, and my little pen that stood on its end, and the box of tissue above my bed for cleaning my reading glasses at night, and my shitty, shitty job—

LOMY

    Listen to yourself. Those were props. That was a character you were playing.

EICHERSEN

    My character. Mine.

LOMY

    I am—trying very hard here not to take this the wrong way.

EICHERSEN

    No, please—take it the wrong way, please. Take this the absolutely worst way you can. I don't—like you, Lomy. OK? I never did. But at least I thought, however crazy and misguided, I thought that you were a person of honorable intentions. Sort of a—a bad Samaritan. Now; now I see you're nothing more than a thief, a scam artist.

LOMY

    Man; you and your fucking property. You think you own this? You think this is yours? Here. Take the fucking shirt. It's a fucking shirt. It's not your fucking soul, man. It's not your fucking soul!

EICHERSEN

    Put the shirt back on.

LOMY

    I don't want it! I don't want to be part of you.

EICHERSEN
Please don't take your clothes off in here.

LOMY
This is a great story. A guy, a simple guy, is pulled out of his pointless life, and raised to greatness, so that he can what? Ask for his pants back? That's a great story. That's an awe-inspiring, that's a—

EICHERSEN
I'm not asking for my pants back.

LOMY hands EICHERSEN his pants.

Thank you.

Beat.

You can have these.

LOMY
I don't want them.

EICHERSEN
This isn't about pants.

LOMY
Oh, I think it is.

EICHERSEN
I'm asking for my life back.

LOMY
You have so completely missed the point of this.

EICHERSEN
No, no. I think I have finally seen the point of this. You don't want to change the world.

LOMY
No?

EICHERSEN
You want to run away to the Caribbean with my girlfriend.

LOMY
: Listen to yourself.

EICHERSEN
: You had me completely fooled. I thought you were crazy. You're not crazy at all. You're an opportunist, Lomy. Plain and simple. You know something. I kind of half-believed you there for a bit. I kind of, maybe just a small part of me, thought you were legitimately trying to do something for me. Because, OK, I'll admit, I wanted somebody to do something for me. If we get right down to it. If we dig deep enough, I suppose. I wanted, yes, something out of it. Maybe some sort of kick, maybe some sort of charge.

LOMY
: So, the hundred dollars wasn't charity. Is that what you're saying?

EICHERSEN
: I thought we were way past that.

LOMY
: You were trying to buy something?

EICHERSEN
: I don't know. Isn't that what charity is? Trying to buy something? Forgiveness or gratitude or temporary unimpeded passage.

LOMY
: I am so disappointed in you.

EICHERSEN
: Good.

LOMY
: You inspired me to greatness, Oswald. Not just me: others. It's why you were going to give the speech.

EICHERSEN
: Speech?

LOMY
: Here. Tomorrow night.

EICHERSEN
What are you—?

LOMY
I only handed out a few leaflets, sure, but word is spreading. There's going to be a crowd here tomorrow night. What the fuck am I supposed to tell them?

EICHERSEN
Leaflets.

LOMY
That the guy who inspired us all with his unparalleled kindness and his generosity was only trying to buy temporary unimpeded passage?

EICHERSEN
Yes, that's right.

LOMY
The sky is opening up, man. The sky. Opening up. And behind it, a stream of brilliant sunlight, pouring out over this frozen wasteland of indifference and fucking ice, and cracking it wide open.

Producing a crude handbill.

Look at this. Look.

EICHERSEN
"Albert Pennyfarthing, great thinker and liberator, speaks tomorrow night on the subject of Benevolence. Foxy Triple-X. Eight p.m. Restricted."

LOMY
We had to put that because of the venue.

Beat.

EICHERSEN
I don't care what it says. I'm not giving a speech, on Benevolence, or any other subject.

LOMY
And what am I supposed to tell all these people when they show up? That you wanted your shirt back? That

goodness doesn't really exist after all. That we can all
return to our shitty little corner of the Earth and keep
begging?

EICHERSEN
I don't believe a word you're saying, Lomy. I don't
believe a word of it.

LOMY
It's not about believing me.

EICHERSEN
No?

LOMY
The sky is opening up. The fucking sky.

EICHERSEN
I'll tell you one thing that's opened up—I mean, besides
my bank account. I have opened up. You have awoken in
me anger and vengeance. Not against the world—against
you.

LOMY
OK. Then here.

*He hands EICHERSEN his gun. EICHERSEN turns it in his
hand.*

You know what a gun is? Just an extension of a thought.
Not even a thought. Bang. Do it.

EICHERSEN
Don't test me, Lomy.

LOMY
I have to say, Oz, for an inspirational figure, you are
seriously lacking in leadership qualities. And if you don't
shoot me, I'm just going to have to shoot myself, because
I am so disappointed in you. So very disappointed. If you
didn't want to be this person, then why didn't you just
pass me by? Why didn't you just give me a fucking
quarter and pass me by like everybody else?

EICHERSEN
>Get out of my life.

LOMY
>You get out of my life. Leave me be, man. Quit passing me by all the time. Quit going in and out of doors I can't go in and out of. Quit not looking at me, and wishing I wasn't there. Get away from me. Get away from my heart and my soul. I don't want to feel anything for you. I don't want to believe in anything anymore—not you, not anything. Kill me now, because I am dead to you anyway.

EICHERSEN
>We're all dead to each other.

LOMY
>Is that what you think? Is that what you really think?

EICHERSEN
>I'm just so angry.

LOMY
>Are you? Then do something, for fuck's sake.

EICHERSEN
>Why have you done this?

LOMY
>This isn't the time for questions. Give me that.

>*LOMY grabs for the gun, they struggle.*

EICHERSEN
>No.

LOMY
>Give—it.

>*A shot is fired. They look at one another.*
>*Blackout.*

Scene Eight

AUDREY sits beside EICHERSEN, saying nothing for a beat.

EICHERSEN
So, how is he?

AUDREY
It doesn't look good.

EICHERSEN
But you spoke with him?

AUDREY
Briefly. He's in and out of—what's it called.

EICHERSEN
Consciousness?

AUDREY
Rooms. They can't seem to find a room for him. Anyway, he's under police protection.

EICHERSEN
Why?

AUDREY
I suppose they feel he's threatened.

EICHERSEN
By who? Himself?

AUDREY
Not exactly. They're pinning the whole thing on you.

EICHERSEN
Me?

AUDREY
>Incredulity doesn't suit you, Ozzie.

EICHERSEN
>No?

AUDREY
>You told me you wanted to kill him. What else was I supposed to tell the police?

EICHERSEN
>You told the police I wanted to kill him?

AUDREY
>Didn't you?

EICHERSEN
>Only in a manner of speaking.

AUDREY
>A bullet in the chest is hardly a manner of speaking.

EICHERSEN
>Audrey, you have to believe me.

AUDREY
>I don't know what to believe anymore. I'm beginning to think that Lomy might have been a mistake. Without Dr. Strauss around it's—so confusing.

EICHERSEN
>Yeah?

AUDREY
>Sometimes it's hard to tell the difference between sexual charisma and full-blown insanity.

EICHERSEN
>I thought—the two of you—

AUDREY
>It's over. I mean, if he lives.

EICHERSEN
>Oh.

AUDREY

Let's face it; it's time you and I both admitted to our shortcomings.

Beat.

You go first.

Beat.

Alright, let me say it for you. You let people walk all over you.

EICHERSEN

Who? Besides Lomy and, OK, my sales manager, and the dry cleaning lady—but that's—

AUDREY

Me. You let me walk all over you.

EICHERSEN

Well, you don't have to.

AUDREY

Ozzie, that is, that is so sweet and so sad. Of course I have to.

EICHERSEN

OK, let's talk about your shortcomings. You walk all over people.

AUDREY

That is not a shortcoming.

EICHERSEN

Alright. How about, you had an affair with a crazy street person.

AUDREY

In my own defence, I didn't see it.

EICHERSEN

You didn't see that he hasn't washed his hair for five years?

AUDREY
I was blinded by lust. Alright, I wasn't blinded by it, I had my eyes open to it. But to what? It won't happen again.

EICHERSEN
No?

AUDREY
Sure, we all have an underneath side. But I just don't want to know. We're going to forget this chapter of our lives. I am not going to the Grand Caymans to launder stolen money, I am not going to have sex with a panhandler regardless of his other—endowments—whatever those might be, and I am not, I am not going to allow myself to be swept away by any man, no matter how tragic or desperate. And you, Oswald, are going to stop all this business of hiding out from the law in a porn theatre.

EICHERSEN
You think we can just return to the indifference of our everyday lives?

AUDREY
We can try.

EICHERSEN
I shot a guy.

AUDREY
Not complete indifference. But we have to manage and organize our feelings in such a way that we don't—indifference, Oswald, is all that saves us from ourselves.

EICHERSEN
I'm a wanted man.

AUDREY
Not—that wanted.

The regular PATRON enters, sits.

Oh, for heaven's sake.

EICHERSEN
> What?

AUDREY
> That man.

EICHERSEN
> He's not hurting anyone.

AUDREY
> Honestly.

EICHERSEN
> Besides, they've stopped showing dirty pictures.

AUDREY
> So, what's he doing here?

EICHERSEN
> The world is a lonely place.

AUDREY
> You think he's looking for companionship?

EICHERSEN
> I don't know what people are looking for. Do you know what people are looking for, Audrey?

AUDREY
> Oh, Oswald, don't ask those questions. You know I hate it when you ask those questions.

EICHERSEN
> Am I being picayune?

AUDREY
> I'm getting another dog.

EICHERSEN
> I don't—like dogs.

AUDREY
> What do you mean?

EICHERSEN
> I mean I don't like dogs. You should know that, Audrey. Once and for all. Before we—if we ever intend to—to—

AUDREY
>We're not getting back together. Is that what you think? We're not getting back together.

EICHERSEN
>No?

AUDREY
>For one thing, the police are after you, which does not bode well for our future. And besides, Ozzie, you've given me an insight into myself that I never had before. Men are awful.

EICHERSEN
>That's—not really an insight into yourself.

AUDREY
>I think it is. I attach myself to men. I think I need them. I don't. They're hopeless, useless appendages. Thank you for helping me to see that.

EICHERSEN
>You're—welcome.

>*She stands; the PATRON shifts his position.*

AUDREY
>Anyway, I'm sort of inspired now to go out and do some good in the world.

EICHERSEN
>Oh?

AUDREY
>Commercial real estate really does help people in need.

EICHERSEN
>By "people in need," you mean rich people.

AUDREY
>They can't help it if they have money.

EICHERSEN
>Poor things.

>*He stands.*

>Audrey. Can we just—hug each other for a moment?

AUDREY
No.

Beat.

Here?

EICHERSEN
Here.

They hug awkwardly.

AUDREY
I have to go.

Beat.

EICHERSEN
Audrey, everything I have, everything I ever had, ever was, has been taken away from me. I'm—somebody else. And I don't know who that is.

AUDREY
I've changed, too, Ozzie. Inside I've changed. And it's just going to make me a stronger salesperson.

EICHERSEN
Great.

AUDREY
Do you need some money? Normally I wouldn't, but if it'll help me feel a little better about leaving you—

EICHERSEN
If you wouldn't mind, Audrey—

AUDREY rustles through her purse, finding her wallet and pulling out bills.

AUDREY
Here. It's a hundred dollars. Don't ever say I'm lacking in irony.

She goes; on her way out she runs into JACKIE, entering.

JACKIE
Oh. Hello.

AUDREY
    He's all yours.

JACKIE
    He isn't anybody's.

    She exits. JACKIE comes down the aisle and sits by EICHERSEN. She is dressed, rather uncharacteristically, in a smart business suit.

    What's with her?

EICHERSEN
    Jackie, you look—

JACKIE
    It's a miracle.

EICHERSEN
    Is it?

JACKIE
    Here. He gave me this.

EICHERSEN
    Who?

JACKIE
    Lomy.

EICHERSEN
    You saw him?

    JACKIE hands him a small stone.

    W-what's it for?

JACKIE
    Don't ask me.

EICHERSEN
    Well, I hate it when people give you things like this.

JACKIE
    Throw it away.

EICHERSEN
    You can't just throw it away. It's, it's—

JACKIE
He also has a ticket here for the Cayman Islands for you.

EICHERSEN
Me?

JACKIE
Two tickets, actually. He says you should get lost. He says you should take me with you.

Beat.

I have to get out of town.

EICHERSEN
You do?

JACKIE
I stabbed Archie—in the abdomen. With my styling sheers.

EICHERSEN
Oh, is that—is he dead?

JACKIE
You can't kill a guy like Archie. He's too big; he's, he's everywhere. You just have to run; that's all.

EICHERSEN
He's after you?

JACKIE
No, *you* have to run. He's after you, the big idiot. What do you think of my outfit?

EICHERSEN
Me? Why?

JACKIE
Well, I told him.

EICHERSEN
Told him what?

JACKIE
What you told me, baby.

EICHERSEN
   What did I tell you?

JACKIE
   To stand up for myself.

EICHERSEN
   I never told you that.

JACKIE
   You did. You said that a hooker's life was a wasted life, and that I should go out and really make something of myself.

EICHERSEN
   When did I—?

JACKIE
   The very first time we met.

EICHERSEN
   No, I didn't. A hooker is useful, a hooker is ... Go back and tell him I didn't say that.

JACKIE
   I stood up for myself. That's the important thing. Lomy's right about you.

EICHERSEN
   He's not even slightly right.

JACKIE
   I hope you don't mind that I put the skirt and the jacket on your credit card.

EICHERSEN
   I still have credit; that is a miracle.

JACKIE
   I'm a whole different person, from now on—thanks to you.

EICHERSEN
   I really—I had nothing to do with—anything.

JACKIE
You gave up everything, Ozzie.

EICHERSEN
Not—voluntarily.

JACKIE
You inspired me to walk away from my life, just the way you did. Hold me for a second.

EICHERSEN
Jackie, I—

JACKIE
Don't say anything.

The film starts. They embrace.

I prayed for this to happen.

EICHERSEN
This film?

JACKIE
One day I was with some john in a hotel room, and I had a really bad cold, and I was just looking up at the ceiling—actually, it wasn't the ceiling, come to think of it, it was the floor—but, anyway, I was looking up, and I said, "God, if you get me out of this someday, I will simply have to believe in you." Look, I stole this little cross.

EICHERSEN
God will be so pleased.

JACKIE
I know.

They watch the film.

What is this, anyway?

EICHERSEN
It's Italian.

JACKIE
This isn't a dirty picture?

EICHERSEN
Not if it has subtitles.

JACKIE
Porn is better; this is just creepy.

EICHERSEN
I've never been to the Grand Caymans.

JACKIE
Me neither.

EICHERSEN
Jackie, I don't—really know you.

JACKIE
I don't really know you, either. We're like—two people who don't know each other.

EICHERSEN
Are we?

JACKIE
I'm going to reshape your whole head.

EICHERSEN
Put the scissors away. Listen to me. I can't live in the Cayman Islands; I don't even know where they are.

JACKIE
Does anybody?

EICHERSEN
Well, presumably the pilot. The point is, wherever they are, they're a long way from reality.

JACKIE
Reality? Are you fucking kidding me? Reality?

EICHERSEN
How is the world supposed to work if nobody ever accepts anything?

JACKIE
You said we should never accept.

EICHERSEN
> You see, that's a, that's a very noble, a very reckless and noble idea; I wouldn't have said that. My nobility is a kind of—a kind of—what's the opposite of nobility?

JACKIE
> So, you think I should go back to turning tricks?

EICHERSEN
> No. No.

JACKIE
> You think you can face down Archie?
>
> *Beat.*

EICHERSEN
> What time is the flight?

JACKIE
> You have to take advantage of your opportunities.

EICHERSEN
> So, this is an opportunity: for you.

JACKIE
> They don't happen often in my line of work.

EICHERSEN
> Is that how Lomy saw it?

JACKIE
> Lomy is different. He didn't want to take advantage of you, really.

EICHERSEN
> And you did?

JACKIE
> Naturally.

EICHERSEN
> But—he took everything.

JACKIE
And he gave it all away—to me, mostly. Lomy loves the street. He would never leave that spot. It's his calling, he says.

EICHERSEN
What about my clothes? He took my clothes.

JACKIE
He wanted to feel what it felt like to be you.

The PATRON enters and sits, unnoticed by the other two; he slinks low down into his seat.

I'll go and pack up all my things and meet you at the airport.

EICHERSEN
I just need to—I need to—

JACKIE
Sure, I get it.

EICHERSEN
Do you?

JACKIE
Listen. We don't have to know each other, baby. We just have to care about each other.

EICHERSEN
But, you don't care about me.

JACKIE
You can't take that much away from a person and not feel something for them.

EICHERSEN
That's—gee.

JACKIE
Anyway, it's Lomy's idea. He thinks I need someone to look after me, but I don't feel that way. I'm going to be OK, now.

JACKIE stands.

EICHERSEN
　Jackie—

　　She stops.

　Jackie, I—

JACKIE
　Hey. If you're not there, baby, you won't be.

EICHERSEN
　I—

　　Beat.

JACKIE
　You did a good thing.

EICHERSEN
　Not, not—

JACKIE
　It doesn't matter why.

　　She smiles, a little sadly, exits. EICHERSEN sits for a moment, thinking, as the PATRON watches. EICHERSEN produces the gun. He turns it in his hand for a bit. He stops turning, looks at it for a beat. The PATRON speaks, in a high voice.

PATRON
　The speech.

EICHERSEN
　What?

PATRON
　The speech?

　　The little man stands and walks down the aisle, standing next to EICHERSEN and hands him a leaflet.

　I'm here for the speech.

EICHERSEN
　Oh. That was cancelled. That was—I'm sorry; that's not happening tonight. That's—

　　After a beat the PATRON turns and returns to his place, sitting.

There's no speech.

> *EICHERSEN considers. The PATRON waits. EICHERSEN stands. Clears his throat. He walks to the front of the theatre, and turns facing the man at the back. He sighs.*

I have nothing really to say. In fact, I have nothing period. I lost everything. I was taken advantage of. Well, that's not completely—it turns out there was maybe more to it than that. I did something that I had never done before. I—I decided to act on a feeling. I felt an injustice. I saw a man, a few weeks ago, who needed proper footwear; so I gave him a hundred dollars. I didn't think it was fair, that it was right, for anybody to suffer unnecessary orthotic discomfort simply because he was poor and his job required prolonged periods of standing around. Anyway, let me begin by saying thank you—all—for joining me tonight. If you would, uh—thank you, sir, not masturbate, while I'm—that would be, thanks, appreciated. So, uh. Anyway, my name is Albert Pennyfarthing, and I'm here, tonight, to speak on the subject of Benevolence.

> *Blackout.*
> THE END.